Bernhard Reitsma (Ed.)

Fruitful Minorities

Christians under Pressure:
Studies in Discrimination and Persecution

On behalf of the International Institute for Religious Freedom
edited by Thomas Schirrmacher and Christof Sauer

Volume 1

Vol 1   Bernhard Reitsma (Ed.). Fruitful Minorities – The Witness
and Service of Christian Communities in Predominantly
Islamic Societies

Vol 2   Kay Bascom. Overcomers – God's Deliverance through
the Ethiopian Revolution as Witnessed Primarily by the
Kale Heywet Church community

IIRF

Bernhard Reitsma (Ed.)

Fruitful Minorities

The Witness and Service of Christian Communities in Predominantly Islamic Societies

WIPF & STOCK · Eugene, Oregon

Wipf and Stock Publishers
199 W 8th Ave, Suite 3
Eugene, OR 97401

Fruitful Minorities
The Witness and Service of Christian Communities
in Predominantly Islamic Societies
By Reitsma, Bernhard
Copyright©2018 Verlag für Kultur und Wissenschaft
ISBN 13: 978-1-5326-6314-7
Publication date 7/11/2018
Previously published by Verlag für Kultur und Wissenschaft, 2018

Contents

List of Contributing Authors

Atef Gendy is the president of the Evangelical Theological Seminary in Cairo, Egypt. He also serves as a Professor of New Testament at this seminary. He is a consultant for the Revised Arabic Bible Translation (Van Dyck) and a member of the editorial committee of the Arabic Contemporary Commentary.

Najla Kassab is Director of Christian Education of the National Evangelical Synod of Syria and Lebanon. She is an ordained minister in this denomination. She currently serves as the president of the World Communion of Reformed Churches.

Petrus Sugito is a pastor in the Gereja Kristen Jawa Tengah Utara (GKJTU) in Java, Indonesia, and served his church as a general secretary for many years. He presently works in the United Evangelical Mission as the Deputy Executive Secretary for Asia.

Bernhard Reitsma is professor by special appointment at the Vrije Universiteit Amsterdam for the Church in the Context of Islam and senior lecturer of Missiology and Islam at the Christian University of Applied Science in Ede, the Netherlands.

Lambang Mandi Tandi Pare is a pastor in the Gereja Protestan Indonesia di Luwu (GPIL), and at present chairperson of the GPIL synod. Previously, he served as the chairperson of the Centre for Training and Capacity Development of the GPIL.

Youssef Yacob is a pastor of the Evangelical Church of Algeria. He and his wife are the founders of the House of Hope fellowship and ministries.

Sameh Ibrahim is a pastor of the Presbyterian Church in el-Minia, Egypt, and lecturer of New Testament in the el-Minia branch of the Evangelical Theological Seminary in Cairo.

Rima Nasrallah is an assistant professor of Practical Theology at the Near East School of Theology in Beirut.

Wilbert van Saane is a chaplain and instructor at Haigazian University in Beirut.

Anneta Vyssotskaia trains church leaders in Central Asia and has repeatedly written on the lack of religious freedom in this part of the world.

Andi Dina is a Christian leader, trainer and researcher in Albania. He is a pastor of a local church.

Rik Lubbers is a Dutch missionary in Kosovo, seconded by GZB and ECM (European Christian Mission). He serves the Protestant Evangelical Church in Kosovo.

Herman Takken worked until recently on the staff of Evangelie & Moslims (evangelie-moslims.nl), an organization of several Reformed denominations for witness and service among Muslims in the Netherlands.

Arie van der Poel is regional coordinator of the GZB for the Middle East, North Africa and Central Asia.

GZB, founded in 1901, is a Dutch mission agency within the Protestant Church in the Netherlands (PKN) and supports local churches and Christian organizations across the globe to be living and witnessing communities of faith that share the Gospel in word and deed (www.gzb.nl).

Introduction

Arie van der Poel and Bernhard Reitsma

Background and Purpose of This Book

The idea for this unique book was born in Salatiga, Indonesia, in 2012, during a partner conference organized by the Dutch Protestant mission agency GZB. The conference brought together more than twenty representatives from various Protestant churches in Asia, Africa, Europe and the Middle East. The theme of the conference was "Being Christian in the context of Islam".

A year prior to the Salatiga conference, the GZB had launched its new motto "mission connects" (*zending verbindt*). The vision behind this phrase is that Christians worldwide need each other more than ever as partners in God's mission. They are fundamentally one and need to express their unity in partnership. The conference was intended to do just that. Christians in different parts of the world need each other to learn from each other and encourage each other. They cannot do without each other, because they belong together. That makes them realize that they do not wrestle alone, that others have similar problems, that they are connected to brothers and sisters worldwide on a deep level, and that others draw comfort, faith and hope from the same source. This book intends to document different insights and experiences from different parts of the world in order to inform and encourage Christian communities in different contexts.

During the conference in Salatiga several issues that Christians in the context of Islam encounter surfaced. A recurrent theme was that of being a minority. Many participants belong to Christian communities that are a minority amidst a majority of Muslims and wonder how they can still be fruitful. The authors who have contributed to this book are themselves Christians who live in predominantly Islamic societies or people who have an intimate knowledge of Christianity in such contexts. They have written their texts with the explicit objective to encourage others who find themselves in similar circumstances. The way they think and how they deal with their challenges may be relevant and helpful to other Christians. It is a book that was written in the spirit of partnership.

The contexts described in this book are widely divergent. For example, at Salatiga our eyes were opened to the very different experiences of

Christians in Egypt, where relations between Christians and Muslims are often tense, and those in different parts of Indonesia, where close family ties between Christians and Muslims are no exception.

The Salatiga conference set a process of thinking and visioning in motion. In spite of their different contexts, the participants felt that together we can develop a renewed vision of our calling as Christian churches among and towards our Muslim neighbours. Some of the chapters of this book are reworked presentations from the Salatiga conference, but most chapters were written especially for this book. Some of the case studies date from a few years ago, but their continuing relevance is beyond doubt. Because of different circumstances the editing and processing of these studies required careful attention.

The purpose of this book is to encourage and inspire pastors, elders and other church leaders who serve in a diversity of contexts where Islam is present one way or another. We also hope that the book will find its way into theological seminaries and training institutes and will be used to train and mould the leaders of tomorrow. In short, with this book, we want to serve the church. It is an expression of the fact the Christians in Christ are not on their own, even in the most isolated situations. They constitute a worldwide community of brothers and sisters of which Christ himself is the head.

Identity, Vocation and Praxis

The rediscovery of our vocation and mission must be rooted in a clear vision of our identity. Most partners live as minorities in countries that have Muslim majorities. In some cases, the pressure on the church is high and the challenges manifold. Under pressure, churches cannot ignore profound questions about their identity: Who are we as Christians in this context? Why should we continue to be Christians?

At Salatiga, these questions of identity and vocation were discussed in relation to each other. As the conference progressed, however, the emphasis increasingly fell on vocation. How can we as Christian minorities contribute to our societies and in this way bear fruit? The speakers affirmed that even where Christian minorities have to manoeuvre cautiously, it is more fruitful to use the available space – no matter how small – than continuously emphasize the confrontation between Muslims and Christians. In this way, they rejected an antagonistic approach to Islam.

From this basic sense of vocation, the discussions at Salatiga then focused on the praxis. Is it possible to be a minority in a Muslim majority context and still be a living, vital Christian community? Is it possible to participate in and contribute to the society and have a positive impact that benefits the whole country? Is it possible for such a minority community to explain and demonstrate what the gospel contains and implies? Or is a minority status simply a very negative situation, in which the Christian community finds itself effectively on the side lines of society? In some areas of the world, one can even wonder whether the churches will continue to exist as minorities. In parts of Iraq and Syria, Christianity is close to being wiped out altogether. Will there be any Christian presence left in the future? Is being a minority in itself not a contradiction to being fruitful?

The dangers of the minority status were made very clear at Salatiga. They will also be addressed in this book. It sometimes seems as if the only viable response to the challenge of being a minority is to withdraw into the safety of the church community; Christians go into survival mode. They may even resemble the servant from the parable of Jesus who buried his talent. In this case, the only mission the church has left is to try to survive. This is understandable. One of the most basic drives for human beings is to stay alive and survive. And the best way to survive often seems to hide for danger or to run away from it. This is also true for religious communities. However, withdrawing often only kills even more of the life of the church and the gospel and leads to a further decrease in impact and eventually in numbers. That forces the church again to confront the question of identity.

The reader will find this reflective cycle of *identity - vocation - praxis* as a pattern throughout this book. It is a cycle that progresses and, we hope, leads the reader up a spiral staircase to a beautiful vista: a positive outlook, which reframes our thinking about minorities.

The issue of persecution is not the main theme of this book. The challenges of being a minority are much wider than just persecution. Of course minorities are much more vulnerable for discrimination, exclusion and violence than majorities. In different chapters issues of persecution have therefore been addressed. Yet the focus of the book is on the contribution Christians can give to their societies.

The Concept of Minority

In part one, four different authors from four different perspectives – Egypt, Indonesia, the Netherlands, and Lebanon – share what they have learned from the Bible and the Christian tradition about Christian communities as minorities. In part two the biblical-theological analyses of part one are complemented by case studies. Different writers tell the stories of their "fruitful minorities" in Islamic contexts. They describe how, even in the most difficult circumstances, Christians can still share the love of Christ and be a light to the world around them. That this is not without struggle goes without saying.

As soon as we talk about the church as a minority, we need to clarify what we mean by the term "minority". We are not simply speaking about numbers. There are many other factors that make communities a minority. For instance, we need to be aware that the socio-political situation of Christians as a minority in Indonesia is completely different from that in Egypt.

When we write about Christianity in Europe, we need to clarify that Christians have increasingly become a religious minority. Yet the European churches' minority status is different from that of churches in Egypt and Indonesia. Although in Europe church membership has decreased substantially over the last fifty years, the church is a minority in a postmodern, often secular context, whereas the churches in Egypt and Indonesia are minorities in the midst of an Islamic majority. Secularism is not part of these contexts in the same way as it is in Europe.

It is obvious that we have to be aware of the specific contexts in which Christians live, but it is exactly this diversity of context that provides the contrast that helps us to learn lessons from each other, which we can subsequently apply in our own context. We believe that the reflections in this book will also be helpful for Christians who are not living among a majority of Muslims. The encounter with the Islamic community has somehow brought to surface basic principles of being church in the world, whatever the context. It is exactly the minority situation that urges Christians to rethink these basic principles of identity.

During our conference and the process of writing and editing this book we have gained more insight in a specifically Christian understanding of minority. We are aware of theories about religious minorities designed by social scientists. In this book, these theories will play only a marginal role. We are also aware that within some strands of Islam the Christian community is regarded as *ahl al dhimma*, a minority by principle, regardless of numbers. The notion of *dhimma* will occur frequently throughout the book and, if not mentioned explicitly, will be not far below the surface. However, from the different contributions a specific understanding of minority will emerge, which is, we trust, founded on a shared interpretation of the Bible and understanding of the history of Christianity. The authors, who are all from Protestant and Evangelical backgrounds, have attempted to anchor their definitions of minority in

Scripture and many also take the history of the church into considera-tion. This is especially the case in part one of the book; it is less explicit in the case studies, but not entirely absent.

Our focus is thus not primarily on numbers, on counting Christians – although we do not deny the importance of this – but on the *attitude* with which the church occupies its place in society. We try to reframe the concept of minority in a biblical and theological way and we are con-vinced that being a minority in that light can actually be a positive con-cept.

We thank André Harris for copy-editing this book.

A Fruitful Minority

Biblical Reflections in the Context of the Evangelical Church of Egypt

Atef Gendy

The History of the Egyptian Church in a Nutshell

The Coptic Orthodox Church of Egypt is an ancient church. It traces its origins back to the supposed coming of Saint Mark the Evangelist to Alexandria, in 70 AD. The Coptic tradition states that Mark came with broken sandals and that the cobbler who fixed his shoes was not only the first convert to Christianity in Egypt, but also the first Patriarch of Alexandria. The church expanded rapidly and by the fourth century, Egypt was a "Christian country". It seems that from the beginning, Christianity was contextualized in Egypt, in worship and Bible translations that appeared even in local Coptic dialects. Alexandria was an important theological centre; its catechetical school, established in 190 AD, was influenced by theologians such as Athanasius, Clement of Alexandria, and the great Origen. They were great apologetic defenders of the Christian faith against Gnosticism and other heresies. The theologian Athanasius was important for Christianity, since his thinking is behind much of the Nicene Creed. He was also able to distinguish the inspired books of the scriptures from the false ones. The twenty-seven New Testament books he identified later became the canon of the New Testament.

Egypt was invaded by the Arab Muslims in 639 and finally conquered with the fall of Alexandria in 641, during the rule of the second caliph of Islam, Umar Ibn Al-Khattab. Because of the harsh conditions for the Coptic Church under Roman rule – the church was often persecuted and counted numerous martyrs – many Christians helped the invading armies. Through the first centuries after the conquest, the church of Egypt still flourished. As long as Christians paid the *dhimmi* tax, the *jizya*, they possessed relative freedom of religion. Rich Christians were able to pay the tax, poor ones had to convert to Islam or be persecuted and killed.

From the beginning of the second millennium, things started to change and Copts became more and more restricted in their religious life and worship. By the end of the twelfth century, because of conversion and a high birth rate among Muslims, the demography of the country had changed so much that a predominantly Christian country had changed into a predominantly Muslim country. The Coptic minority now had an inferior position to the Muslim majority. In the early nineteenth century the situation began to improve again and in due time the jizya was lifted. Nevertheless, Copts remained a Christian minority in an Islamic state.

For Sunni Islam, Egypt has always been important. If Mecca is the heart of Islam, than Cairo can certainly be called the mind of Islam. The centre of education and of spiritual guidance in Sunni Islam is Al-Azhar University, which is one of the oldest religious educational institutes in the world. This leading university in the Islamic world teaches not only Islam and Islamic law, but all major subjects of regular universities. Every year, Al-Azhar graduates many Islamic scholars, muftis, imams and other spiritual leaders from all over the world.

American Protestant missionaries came to Egypt in 1854. Since as foreigners they were not allowed to buy or possess any land, they used a boat (the *Ibis*) as their base to reach villages alongside the river Nile. The boat became the centre of the mission and sailed the Nile from North to South. Since the majority of Egyptians lived and still live in the Nile Delta and along the river, their boat enabled the missionaries to cover almost the entire country. However, the expected influx of converts from Islam did not materialize. The main source of new Protestant Christians was the Coptic Orthodox Church. According to the CIA World Fact Book, Christians in Egypt make up approximately 10 percent of the total population of around 88.5 million people.

The "Arab Spring": Concerns and Fears of Egyptian Christians

The Arab Spring started on 17 December 2010 in Tunisia, when Muhammad Bouazizi set himself on fire in protest of poverty and oppression. His death sparked a movement of protest that spread around the Arab world. Unfortunately, in different places like Libya, Syria and the Gulf-states the movement was hijacked by either tribal interests or Sunni-Shia divisions. In Egypt, mass protests against the regime of President Hosni Mubarak eventually led to his removal from office on 11 February 2011. The elections that followed were a sign of new freedom and democracy. They brought to power the Muslim Brotherhood party in June 2012, which slowly seized more power at the expense of other political groups, including Christians. One year later a second revolution ended the Brotherhood's regime. The army took over again in order to prepare for new elections. Eventually, with the support of the majority of the Egyptian people, including many Christians, General Abdel Fattah al-Sisi became the new president of Egypt in June 2014.

The events in Egypt have changed Egyptian society in many ways. On the one hand, recent developments brought more freedom for Christians. After the first revolution, Christians and Muslims worked together for a new society, despite several incidents between different groups. When the police collapsed, Muslims protected Christians and Christian churches, while Christians supported Muslims. After the elections in which the Muslim Brotherhood gained victory, many Christians feared more restrictions on the freedom of worship, the building and restoration of churches and church properties, restrictions on Christian activities, the imposition of Islamic dress code on Christian women and the implementation of the dhimmi laws and jizya taxes. From the start of the Brotherhood government, moderate Muslim Egyptians complained of bans on cultural and liberal arts, harsher discrimination against women, intensified Islamic education and culture through schools and media, and the restriction of tourism.

After the second revolution, there has been both joy and fear. The aggression against Christians and Christian churches immediately after the ousting of the Muslim Brotherhood shows the vulnerability of Christians as a minority, especially when the government fails to act on behalf of all citizens and fails to preserve democracy and human rights. At the same time, there is a new freedom and openness, as well as new relationships between Muslims and Christians.

The future is unpredictable, especially in light of the rise of violence and the spread of fundamentalism across the region through the Islamic State (ISIS), Al-Qaeda and other extremist groups. Some fear an "Arab Winter" for Christians, while others see new and unprecedented possibilities. So far, Egypt still has the largest Christian minority in the Middle East, but nobody knows what will come.

Biblical Reflections on the Church as a Minority

Being a minority church in Egypt among a majority of Muslims is not simply a negative reality. The church's minority status adds new elements of Christian identity and addresses the church in six different areas. The minority position challenges the church:

1) to recalculate the *influence* of a minority church:
   a theology of *power*;

2) to rethink *the nature* of a minority church:
   a theology of *incarnation*;
3) to remember the *call* of a minority church:
   a theology of the *cross*;
4) to recall the *hope* of a minority church:
   a theology of the *resurrection*;
5) to revisit the *gospel* a minority church brings to the world:
   a theology of *mission*;
6) to revisit the *message* of the church in the world of Islam:
   a theology in *context*.

(1) A theology of power: recalculating the influence of a minority church

The fact that the church is a minority reminds us that the power of the Christian community is of a different quality than political, economic or religious power. The gospel is not forcing itself upon others with competing power and strength, rivalling the different forces in society. It comes to the world in weakness. Jesus says that his kingdom is not of this world, and so his servants do not fight for him (John 18:36). He is a king who conquers by dying for his enemies (John 19:19). The power of the church is defined and qualified by the cross of Christ. Christ's power is made perfect in weakness; if the church is weak, then it is strong (2 Cor 12:9). The nature of the life of the church in this world is always ambivalent. "We have" this "in jars of clay, to show that the surpassing power belongs to God and not to us" (2 Cor 4:6 and 7 ESV). That means that "we are afflicted in every way, but not crushed; perplexed, but not driven to despair; persecuted, but not forsaken; struck down, but not destroyed; always carrying in the body the death of Jesus, so that the life of Jesus may also be manifested in our bodies" (2 Cor 4:8-10 ESV). Being a minority, the church needs to rediscover the meaning of these verses for a life among a Muslim majority. It implies that the influence of the church in society does not depend on its power or social status, but only on the presence of the light of God's glory in the face of Christ, shining through weak human vessels.

(2) A theology of incarnation: rethinking the nature of the church

The nature of the church as a minority is determined by the incarnation of the Word of God. The incarnation is not just a rational doctrine, but should also be something very real in the life of the church in the world of Islam. Christ is the Word that became flesh (John 1:14), the only beloved Son at the Father's side, who has made him known (John 1:18). Because in every respect Christ has been tempted as we are, yet without sin, he is able to sympathize with our weaknesses (Heb 4:15). As the only Son of the Father, the heir of all things, Christ did not come to overpower the world with his heavenly glory and with an army of angels. He laid down his glory and became a vulnerable human being (*kenosis*) and suffered at the hand of the rulers of this world. "Son though he was, he learned obedience from what he suffered and, once made perfect, he became the source of eternal salvation for all who obey him" (Heb 5:8-9).That salvation is the life of the church and is expressed in the Christian community that is an incarnation of Christianity in the Islamic world. Incarnation in this respect means embodying the life of Christ. That also requires *kenosis*, dispensing with one's comfort as the ultimate goal of living. Incarnation means living people's hardships and challenges, identifying with the weak and fighting against injustice. The gospel is at odds with the health, wealth and prosperity "gospel".

(3) A theology of the cross: remembering the call of the church

Embodying the life and the salvation of Christ is equal to representing Christ to the Islamic world. Since the cross was God's way and power of salvation (Rom 1:16), embodying Christ to the world also involves carrying the cross. Following Christ is only possible if one is willing to deny oneself and pick up one's cross daily and follow Christ (Luke 9:23). In this respect, the cross is not just a symbol of suffering, it is a symbol of death. Carrying the cross entails dying to self, to one's personal desires and the expectations of the community. That in turn could easily lead to suffering and persecution at the hands of that community. Thus, authentic Christianity does not exist without the cross. To carry the cross, Christians obviously are not called to commit suicide, seek trouble, or ask for problems. When trouble, however, becomes part of their lives at certain times, they should pray that they are willing and able to carry the cross.

(4) A theology of the resurrection: recalling the hope of the church

The cross is not the final destiny of the church. Christ was called to go to the cross in order to save the world from shame and sin, but his death was not the end. The cross can only be understood in its proper meaning in light of the resurrection. The resurrection reveals what the cross has accomplished. This is the ultimate destiny of Christ and of those who live in him. Christian theology is not simply a theology of martyrdom, which

may inspire others. Rather, it is a theology of resurrection, which proclaims that God has overcome all his enemies and has achieved victory
over sin and death. Therefore, Christians who are a minority and suffer as
a consequence of their faith should have hope, even when they face persecution and death. A theology of resurrection challenges Christians to
actively participate in transforming the current frustrating hopeless situation into a hopeful one. Therefore, Christians should not keep complaining about their circumstances. Unfortunately, sometimes they
grumble more than others about all the problems in the Islamic world
today. Christianity, however, has a specific answer to the concrete needs
and aspirations of the Egyptian people, who are complaining about corruption, the breaking down of values, the uncertainty of life in Egypt and
of the political and economic future. The situation in Egypt after the revolutions is indeed unpredictable and uncertain. Yet Christians have good
reason to be hopeful and they should radiate that hope to the hopeless
people of Egypt, Christians and Muslims alike.

(5) A theology of mission: revisiting the gospel a minority church brings to the world

Being a minority church urges the church to revisit the gospel it is bringing to the world. Jesus went from village to village preaching the gospel
of the Kingdom, casting out demons and healing the sick. And he sent his
disciples to do exactly the same (see Mark 6:13, Matt 10:8 and Luke 10:9).
This raises the question of whether the verbal communication of the
coming of God's kingdom is sufficient. The gospel is never only a verbal
gospel, or only a social gospel. It is a holistic gospel. Just to say that God's
kingdom is near, or that God rules over human life, does not necessarily
carry good news. It is terrible news for sinners and those who rebel
against God! People can only be changed when they *see* the life of the
kingdom, witness the mercies of God in the life of the followers of Jesus.
When they experience the love and care of serving people, they can be
touched by the love of Christ. Only then they will realize that the life
within the kingdom is not boring or terrible, but wonderful. In this way,
it is wrong to speak about two ways of mission, as if some preach and
others live the gospel. It is a complementary mission.

(6) A theology in context: revisiting the message of the church in the Islamic world

In what way does the gospel provide what Muslims need? How can the church communicate the gospel in such a way that the Islamic community is able to understand and accept its message without compromising the essence of the gospel? How can the gospel become at home in the Islamic world so that Muslims can really hear the true gospel reverberating in their own world?

One way to achieve this is to emphasize the distinctiveness of Christianity. What specific concepts does Christianity offer in comparison with Islam? Non-Christians usually appreciate and love to hear about these concepts. As Evangelicals, we generally stress the following ideas that are unique to Christianity.

- Christianity offers an intimate relationship with God.
- Christianity proclaims God as a loving God, not just as a great God.
- Christianity stands for the rights and equality of men and women based on the theology of creation and the theology of redemption.
- Christianity emphasizes the (equal) value of all human beings as created in the image of God, regardless of colour, ethnicity, religion or gender.
- Christianity teaches that God changes human beings inwardly and outwardly, whereas other religions emphasize the practice of rituals.
- Christianity brings hope and assurance of eternal life, in such a way as not even some prophets believed for themselves.
- Christianity's idea of loving one's neighbour is unique, especially in the way Jesus taught it.
- Christianity insists on unlimited forgiveness, another idea that is unique to Jesus' teaching.

In another way, however, a contextual message surfaces in the way we communicate the whole gospel in every area of life. The presence of Christ is more than filling the gaps that Islam has left. It is bringing the fullness of life to people who might have a zeal for God, but lack knowledge (Rom 10:2).

Conclusion: Rethinking Our Minority Status

Christians should rethink their position as minorities, since their minority status can reveal the essence of the gospel more clearly. Being a minority is therefore not necessarily something against God's will. It corresponds in some way to the character of the gospel itself. Christ did not come to establish his kingdom with power, to destroy his enemies, but to save them (Luke 9:56). He did not come to be served, but to serve and to give his life as a ransom for many (Mark 10:45). Christians should therefore not seek to remove the minority status, but instead embrace it as a context for testifying to the heart of the gospel: the incarnation, the death and the resurrection of Jesus Christ. It should be an opportunity to embody the love of Christ to people, even to those we do not like and ultimately to our enemies.

One of the pitfalls minorities face is an exclusive focus on their own situation. Minorities tend to see only their own plight and stand up for their own rights only. But injustice is injustice, whoever it concerns. As a minority, Christians should sympathize with all victims of injustice and persecution. Since God is just, Christians are called to stand up for justice for anyone. The church should speak out against injustice in the name of Christ, even when it concerns their enemies or when it might endanger their own position.

Questions

(1) What does thinking of the church as a minority imply for the West, where Christians are sometimes still a majority?

(2) Is embracing a minority position as an expression of the gospel of Christ tantamount to submitting to a dhimmi-status? That is the critique often heard from people who have an antagonistic approach to Islam. They retort that to embrace a minority status is an unjustified biblical explanation of the claims of political Islam and a submission to them.

(3) At the Cairo Evangelical Theological Seminary, a Professor in Ethics conducted a survey among Muslims and Christians on the top three vices. Interestingly, all Christians and Muslims agreed. The top three vices were: first, to kill someone; second, to commit adultery and, third, to change your religion. What do you think of that? What are the implications of this for Christianity in the Muslim world?

Can You Drink the Cup I Drink?

A Reformed Understanding of Power and Justice in Islamic Contexts

Najla Kassab

Multiple Interpretations of Power and Justice

The words power and justice are overused and have become burdened with several meanings and interpretations. Because of all that is happening related to dominion and power, people use the same words, but refer to totally different realities. This is one of the difficulties of multi-religious societies: concepts like power are used by different religious groups, and each understands them differently.

In the Middle Eastern context, one can hardly separate religious experience from daily perceptions. Discourses are greatly affected by religious teachings. Does a Muslim or a Jew who uses the words power and justice mean the same as a Christian? For Muslims and Jews, what is applicable to their people may not be applicable to those outside their religion. The Islamic teaching about brotherhood, in particular, affects how Muslims perceive power and understand justice. Is justice restricted to the Islamic community? How do Muslims deal with people outside Islam?

A Reformed Understanding of Power and Justice

This is why I find it essential to first unfold the Christian, and more precisely the Reformed, understanding of power. How do we, as the Reformed Church in the Middle East, understand power? To answer that question, I will focus on the discussion between Jesus and his disciples James and John on the road from Bethsaida to Jerusalem, as depicted in Mark 10:35-45. This text helps us to understand what Jesus taught about power. It seems that the issue of power among the disciples was at stake from the beginning. The text reads:

> Then James and John, the sons of Zebedee, came to him. "Teacher," they said, "we want you to do for us whatever we ask." "What do you want me to do for you?" he asked. They replied, "Let one of us sit at your right and the other at your left in your glory." "You don't know what you are ask-

ing," Jesus said. "Can you drink the cup I drink or be baptized with the baptism I am baptized with?" "We can," they answered. Jesus said to them, "You will drink the cup I drink and be baptized with the baptism I am baptized with, but to sit at my right or left is not for me to grant. These places belong to those for whom they have been prepared." When the ten heard about this, they became indignant with James and John. Jesus called them together and said, "You know that those who are regarded as rulers of the Gentiles lord it over them, and their high officials exercise authority over them. Not so with you. Instead, whoever wants to become great among you must be your servant, and whoever wants to be first must be slave of all. For even the Son of Man did not come to be served, but to serve, and to give his life as a ransom for many."

In Mark's version of the story, James and John came to Jesus with a request. They asked him to allow one of them to sit on the right side and the other on the left side of Jesus in his glory. This request was open to different interpretations. Some saw it as an organizational matter, while others thought of it as pure ambition. Still, no matter what the reasons were, no matter if they themselves asked the question or if their mother did, as in Mathew 20:21: either way their request betrayed their understanding of power. This is why Jesus tried to correct their perception of power. Jesus posed them a counter-question, thereby allowing them to rethink their request: "You do not know what you are asking. Are you able to drink the cup that I drink, or to be baptized with the baptism with which I am baptized?"(Mark 10:38 RSV)

If we reflect closely on the events of this story, we find the following. First: the request of the disciples happened on the road to Jerusalem, when Jesus was heading towards the cross. The disciples were not unaware of this, as Jesus had given them clues as to what was going to happen to him. "The Son of Man will be delivered over to the chief priests and the scribes, and they will condemn him to death and deliver him to the Gentiles; and they will mock him and spit upon him, and scourge him and kill him and after three days he will rise." (Mark 10:33-34 RSV) The request of James and John came at a time of unrest. Those who followed Jesus were afraid. As a result, the disciples were confused about what Jesus was saying on the road. Things seemed mixed up to them. They believed that Jesus was to be crowned king. Therefore, they did not understand what Jesus meant when he talked about glory. Had James and John understood Jesus, they would not have asked for prominent positions in his glory. Who among us wants to sit at the left and right hand of a person going to the cross?

Second, it is interesting to note Jesus' answer. He did not rebuke them but, as usual, responded to their question with another question. "Can you drink the cup that I drink, and be baptized with the same baptism?" James and John claimed that they could. Jesus used two metaphors from Jewish life: the metaphor of the cup and the metaphor of baptism. When a king gave his guests a cup, it was considered a symbol of him passing on his experience to them. It was as if Jesus was asking them if they were ready to share his experience and take over the cup from him. Were they prepared to be immersed and baptized in pain with him and face hatred and death? Believe me, Jesus said to them, you do not know what you are asking for. To sit on the right and left of Jesus is to accept the cup and be immersed in pain. At the end of the story, we recognize that the journey of carrying the cup in fact started when the other disciples became angry with James and John for their personal request for power. Jesus clarifies that true power is continuing the experience that Jesus went through. It is to serve and not be served. "Whoever would be first among you must be slave of all. For the Son of man also came not to be served but to serve, and to give his life as a ransom for many." (Mark 10:44-45 RSV)

This is the model of power that Jesus explained to his disciples. Jesus shakes the disciples' concept of power as gaining status. Power that is Christ-like has nothing to do with a superior status; it is the opposite. In Jesus' paradigm, power is the loss of status. It is not only that you do not control people, but also that you serve others and give your life for them. And when people are given a special position and status, it is for the purpose of serving others.

This is a disturbing model of power. It sounds alien to the way power is perceived in the world today and in other religions. It is greatness that stems from servanthood. Power as status divides nations and families and churches, while Jesus' model of power as servanthood unites. I believe this is the main struggle that the church faces today: the Christ model of power against a worldly understanding of power based on status. In the world, having power means taking rather than giving, being served rather than serving. In this model, one gains status through excluding and even killing others. The Christ model advocates the opposite: giving rather than taking, serving rather than being served, including rather than excluding.

The First Challenge: Be True to the Christian Identity

Even though they had spent a considerable time with Jesus, the disciples were confused when it came to power. Jesus made it clear to them that their model was derived from the gentiles. He challenged their concept of power in three ways. We will now reflect on these three challenges that are still relevant to Christians who live in a multi-religious context.

The main challenge for a minority living in a multi-religious society is to be true to its own identity and teachings, and safeguard itself from beliefs that are adapted from external models of power. This is what happened to the disciples in Mark. They were confused by models drawn from outside. The church living in a minority context is called to stick to the paradigm of power that stems from Jesus' teaching. It must be careful not to slide into teachings that may sound attractive but that are not Christian. The world around us sees power as gaining, whereas the Christian understanding of power is emptying oneself, giving and sharing what one has, even if that leads to the cross.

One day in a meeting of leaders of our church, a pastor stood up and made a confession. We had just heard of attacks carried out against the Islamic State (ISIS), in which several ISIS fighters were killed. He said: "I have a confession to make. I was angry with myself when I found myself happy when I saw pictures of dead ISIS members." Our teaching is easily affected and at times even distorted by what happens around us.

In the midst of war and oppression our integrity is easily distorted. We risk sliding into models that are alien to our Christian teaching. As a small minority seeking to be faithful to Christ, we need to keep scrutinizing our beliefs in the light of the word. The church must not give way to the forces around it, or adopt a reactionary attitude. This is the task of individuals as well as communities.

In his famous sermon *Drum Major Instinct,* Martin Luther King Jr. claimed that in each and every one of us there is the instinct to head the procession, to be the drummer who leads the group. King stresses that we should not be too fast to condemn James and John, because we all have the drummer instinct. It is easy to point to others and forget to check our own personal interests and intentions. Again, this is true for individuals and communities.

The church in the Islamic world is called to uphold the Christ-like model of servanthood. This is what makes the church light and salt within a diverse context. We are called to move from concern for our own wellbeing or the wellbeing of our nation to the wellbeing of others; the shalom of others. If we do, justice is lived out. In today's world, the spirit of gaining power and status prevails. This is how countries seek to dominate each other. This is how religious fundamentalists work: they attain status by using violence.

The Second Challenge: Believe That You Can Change Society

The second challenge that minority groups in a multi-religious society face is the belief that a small number is equal to helplessness and weakness. The opposite is true. If a minority church lives up to its teachings and beliefs, and if it focuses on the role it can play in a multi-religious context; then being a numerical minority is not a weakness but a strength. The more the religious community concentrates on its role, the stronger it is: its fear is dispelled. Minorities need not feel helpless or weak, for in spite of their small numbers they can be groups that shape societies and change values. The issue is not an issue of numbers, but an issue of integrity in the life of the community: to walk the talk.

The role of the evangelical church in nineteenth century Lebanon is a case in point. Protestantism had an influence disproportionate to its numbers, for instance on the education of women. Historians have revealed that the education of women in Lebanon was shaped by the educational ministry of the Protestant church. At that time, it was shameful for women to go to school. With love and dedication, the wives of the missionaries taught women in informal ways and sent them to schools. Due to their influence, it became shameful for women *not* to go to school. The dedicated minority was able to change the values of a nation. Nineteenth century Lebanese Protestants were not focused on numbers, but rather on how God could use them in a new way to shape lives. Lebanon would not look the same had it not been for that small, faithful community. It is the servanthood spirit that made all the difference. It is the power of service that can shape others.

As a woman serving in the Presbyterian Church in Lebanon and Syria since 1990, I am challenged daily to consider how God can use me in the life of the church. My focus is on the ways that God can use my talents, not on the limitations that may discourage me. There are many possible sources of discouragement, such as the limited number of women in leadership and the lines that are carefully drawn in the life of the church to define where women can serve. When I focus on the role and when I feel blessed with the way God is using me in the life of the community, my minority feeling turns to majority, my helplessness turns to strength, my fears to confidence. It all starts with my attitude and how I view myself and my role in the eyes of God.

A minority group that accepts its minority status is automatically triggered to serve others outside its borders. The small number pushes the community to think of others. Since its early beginnings in 1824, the evangelical community in Lebanon has focused on serving others in schooling, medical and social services. Although our number is small still we have been able to reach out to huge numbers.

A minority group needs to discover that it can bring about change more easily than a majority group. As a small group, it has the freedom to present new models without threatening others. Small groups can serve as laboratories. They do not immediately affect the general scene. My church is a small group, but we present a model that is different from all other churches and religions in the area. Our non-hierarchical structures, for example, are quite different from other religious groups. The role of the laity in decision-making processes in the church is unique. The decisions are not controlled by one person but by committees. In committees authority is always shared authority. This model is different from any other model in our region. Moreover, our church is a safe testing ground for female leadership in the church. Having women preachers is a very new step that has started to impact other Evangelical churches and groups.

The Third Challenge: Build Bridges of Reconciliation

The third challenge that minorities face is intolerance from the majority. When the majority religion becomes exclusive and radical, minorities are at risk. Fundamentalism in all religions tends to deny the rights and freedoms of others and challenges their beliefs. There are obvious similarities between Christian, Muslim and Jewish fundamentalism. Every fundamentalist group claims to hold the truth and the right to judge or exclude others, or even kill them in the name of true religion. Such fundamentalism is a destructive force that leads the world to chaos.

The rise of ISIS and similar fundamentalist groups is a phenomenon that must be taken seriously. It is leading to the massacre and expulsion of minorities in the Middle East: the Assyrians and Kurds in Syria and the Yezidi people and other minority groups in Iraq. For centuries, different groups have lived side by side; minorities did not feel at risk. It is only when political Islam was strengthened and financially supported that these minorities were confronted by the threat they are facing today.

Living in a multi-religious context can be a blessing and a curse. In peaceful situations, when the rights of minorities are secured and peace prevails, one is enriched by other religions, and one learns to see God in others. However, war, fundamentalism and political agendas distort this beauty. They draw sharp lines between religions and urge every religion to build walls of separation and hatred. Each group thinks of their own status compared to the others and feels intimidated by the other.

As a child growing up in Lebanon, I was raised with Muslim friends and classmates. We children did not know who was a Christian and who a Muslim. All we knew was that we loved our friends and that we sang the same hymns together. It was the war that made us draw lines and build prejudices. We began to guess the religious background of the other children from their names. We lost the beauty of diversity.

Once upon a time two brothers lived on the family farm with their father. Their father grew old and could no longer run the farm. So he called his sons in and told them he was going to split the farm into two: one half for each brother. He knew that they worked well together and that they would always be friends.

The brothers were delighted and worked joyously on their adjacent farms, until one day they got into a big fight and stopped speaking to each other. Years went by and the silence between them grew. Then one day a carpenter knocked on the older brother's door and asked for work. The brother replied, "Yes, I would like you to build a high fence around my property. Start down by the river where my little brother's property meets mine, and please build a very high fence. I do not ever want to see my brother again!"

The eldest brother left the carpenter to work and went into town. When he got back, he was shocked to see that the carpenter had not built a fence at all! Instead the carpenter had built a bridge over the river connecting the two brothers' farms. In disbelief the older brother ran down to the bridge to get a good look at what the carpenter had done. While he was down at the bridge, the younger brother walked towards him. The younger brother said in amazement, "After all the terrible things I have done to you, I cannot believe you built a bridge to welcome me back." He gave his big brother a huge hug.[1]

In the Middle East we are surrounded by hatred and pain. As a minority group we are called to be like the carpenter and build bridges of reconciliation, servanthood and love. If we do, we live out justice and we understand power through the eyes of Jesus. We become fruitful minorities, rejoicing in the ways God uses us to share his love.

---

[1]   Adapted from http://www.sermons4kids.com.

The Challenges of Being a (Christian) Minority in an Islamic Context

Biblical-Theological Reflections

Bernhard Reitsma

Introduction

In many countries, the word minority indicates a group of people that struggles for equal participation in society but often has limited social rights or security. Christians in different areas with a Muslim majority are often such a minority, especially when the political, economic or ethnic situation is unstable. However, there are also different situations. In some countries minorities actually dominate the majority, as used to be the case in Iraq and Syria, and is still the case in Jordan. In most of the Western European countries the situation is different again, for here both Christians and Muslims are minorities in more or less secular societies, but are treated as equal citizens. They are even protected by law against discrimination, even though that does not always guarantee fair treatment.

In this respect, the situation regarding Muslims and Christians in the Netherlands is interesting. Christianity used to be the dominant religion in society for a long time, but has dwindled to officially 40-50 percent of the Dutch population. In reality they number probably no more than 2-3 percent active participants and church membership is still decreasing. This situation leads to concern among Christians for the future of Christianity in the Netherlands. It also creates confusion as to the right response not only to secularization, but to all kinds of new non-institutionalized spirituality – which blends elements from all kinds of religions – as well. And it leads to very diverse responses to the growing presence of Muslims in society.

The Muslim community in the Netherlands is also a minority, numbering around 5-6 percent of the population. However, their situation is quite different: they were almost non-existent in the Netherlands before World War II and grew to nearly one million followers at the present time.[2] The majority of Muslims came to the Netherlands as migrant workers in the 1960s and 1970s, coming predominantly from Turkey and Morocco. Due to their circumstances they could not or were not allowed to participate fully in society. The current second and third generation Muslims have all been born in the Netherlands and, despite persistent discrimination, are Dutch citizens participating in all layers of society. There are also Muslims that came from other parts of the world. Apart from small numbers from Indonesia (after the World War II) and Suriname, many came as refugees from different conflict areas such as Somalia.

In this context Dutch Christians respond in basically two ways to Islam in the Netherlands. There are those Christians who are very concerned that the growing influence of Islam will bring an end to modern democracy and equal rights. They fear that Christians will lose their freedom of religion and become second class citizens. Therefore they intend to fight Islam and regain Christianity's majority power and influence. They either work within the system as long as possible and take key positions in society or try to increase the number of Christians through (sometimes aggressive) evangelism. They engage in a spiritual battle or seek to limit the rights of Muslims and restrict immigration. Others emphasize how much Islam and Christianity have in common, especially when it comes to engaging the major threat of secularism. For that reason, some even want to build a kind of Muslim-Christian coalition. They only fear Muslim extremists.

Those who opt for a fight approach accuse the others of giving in to "dhimmitude", voluntarily accepting a second-class status whenever Muslims would gain power in society. According to Islamic jurisprudence (*fiqh*), Christians belong to the *ahl al dhimma*, the people of the covenant; as *dhimmis* they enjoy religious and political freedom in return for their loyalty to the Muslim community and for paying the dhimmi tax, the *jizya*. In reality, however, the *dhimma* has often implied discrimination and suffering for Christians. If Muslims were to become the majority in the Netherlands, the first group fears this to be the result. Then, the remaining options would be to give in to dhimmitude or to flee Islam by withdrawing into a survival mode and looking for the comfort of eternal life, or by literally running away from Muslims.

---

[2]   Here I am disregarding the fact that the Netherlands had a substantial number of Muslim citizens during the colonial era, when Indonesia, then called the Netherlands Indies, was part of the Kingdom of the Netherlands.

Biblical Reflections

Not only are both approaches bound to fail, they also differ quite substantially from the example of Jesus, who neither ran away from nor
fought the Romans. His willingness to suffer and his death on the cross
demonstrate "most graphically that God does not work through the power structures and ideologies of the world."[3] There is an interesting passage in which Jesus underlines this, while interacting with three people
who want to or are invited to follow him (Luke 9:57-62). Without going
into details, it is clear that Jesus here contrasts allegiance to himself and
life in the kingdom with allegiance to other power structures in the
world, as Kenneth Bailey argues.

The first person is discouraged to follow Jesus because "Foxes have
dens and birds have nests, but the Son of Man has no place to lay his
head." (Luke 9:58). Life in the kingdom—according to Jesus—is a life without possessions. And a life without possessions in the Middle East is a life
with no means to earn respect and honour, and no means to buy allegiance. It becomes impossible to attain any position of power.

The second person asks permission to bury his father before following
Jesus (Luke 9:59). Jesus seems unnecessarily harsh by telling him that it is
up to the dead to bury their own dead; as for those who follow Christ,
they should proclaim the kingdom of God. (Luke 9:60). To understand the
meaning of these words, it is important to know that burying your father
in a Middle Eastern context carries the meaning of looking after your
parents until they die. When Jesus speaks to this man, the situation is not
that his father is about to die or has just passed away and needs a decent
funeral. The man wants to follow Christ only after he has finished his duties to his parents, which is a polite and Middle Eastern way of saying:
"no! There are other, more important things than following you." To Jesus, life in the kingdom implies an unconditional allegiance to him that
surpasses allegiance to earthly systems and bindings.

The third person wants to follow Christ after he has said farewell to
the people at home (Luke 9:61). This seems reasonable, but Jesus denies
him the opportunity, for "no one who puts a hand to the plow and looks
back is fit for the kingdom of God" (Luke 9:62). Here, as in the previous
verses, the Middle Eastern context is important because saying farewell
in a traditional society is more than a simple salutation. It means asking

---

3   Marwa J. Dawn, *A Royal Waste of Time: The Splendor of Worshiping God and Being
Church for the World* (Grand Rapids/ Cambridge: William B. Eerdmans Publishing
Co., 1999), 47.

the head of the family for permission to go. Again, implicitly and very po-litely, this man refuses to follow Jesus, for he knows very well that a de-cent father would never give his son permission to wander around with a nomad like Jesus, with no possessions and no place to go. Jesus stresses that His authority should surpass even the authority of the family, which for a Middle Eastern son is the highest possible earthly authority.

In this passage Jesus clarifies that in the kingdom of God, faith does not easily mix with the power structures of this world (possessions and family). Religion and earthly power do not match, for power always needs force and violence to manifest itself. A religion that strives after power in this world will always end in a form of *jihad*, or expressed in Christian vocabulary—in crusades. The real struggle, according to the New Testament, is not between earthly (economic or political) powers, nor between Christian powers and non-Christian powers, nor between Western so-called democracies and non-Western powers, but between the reign of God, which is not of this world, and everything that tries to obstruct and destroy that kingdom. That inspires us to look at 'being a minority' in a slightly different way.

An Alternative Approach: the Minority Community.[4]

If the church wants to find an alternative to on the one hand trying to regain majority status at the cost of Islam (a fight approach) and suc-cumbing to being a slowly fading minority community on the other, it has to rediscover what it means to be the body of Christ. In spite of its limited numbers, the first church seems to have been a powerful com-munity. Its strength clearly did not depend on large congregations. It cer-tainly did not rely on impressive church buildings, nor on political influ-ence and power. It was exactly because of the absence of an overriding allegiance to the power structures of this world that the first Christians were able to take their place. They did not rely on the powers of the world for their identity and therefore they possessed complete freedom. They had nothing to lose. What they possessed could never be taken away from them. What they had needed not (and could not) be defended with weapons. Precisely because of that, they were able to make a differ-ence in the world.

We could call this the mark of the true community of Christ, reflect-ing Jesus Christ, who claimed that His Kingdom was not of this world, but

---

4   I owe a lot here to Dawn, *A Royal Waste of Time* and Roland Muller, *The Messenger,*
     The Message and the Community (Langley: CanBooks, 2005).

of a different quality. You could say that being a minority here has become an attitude of being present in the world. The church is in that sense always a minority in its attitude and presence in the world, even when it is a numerical majority. I would call that a theological minority. It is the mentality of taking up one's cross and following Christ, of not being overcome by evil, but overcoming evil with good. It is the power received through the empowerment of the Holy Spirit.

When we focus on the community of Christ as the starting point for an alternative approach for the church in the context of Islam, both the Western and the Eastern worlds are challenged. In both contexts, community is a central element in life – albeit in completely opposite ways. One of the main characteristics of the culture of the West, which is usually defined as postmodern, is the disintegration of community life. The collapse of truth and the absence of an all-compassing worldview that could provide coherence to our experience of the world have led to the fragmentation of life and the disappearance of unity. There is no longer one community that serves as a safe haven, but there are many different and varying communities to which people incidentally belong. Communities become groups of changing individuals. In this context, the emphasis on the church as a new community tackles the critical issue head on — providing a new structure of unity and meaning that is built on deeper foundations. The Christian community is the reality of God's new creation. It is called to demonstrate how God intended the world to be. It must exemplify true life in community with God. By being part of this community, people are taken up into this meaning of life and become part of God's story in the world. In this way, the community is God's gift for a postmodern world.

In the – up to the present – still traditional, Middle Eastern society, community is essential in a much more positive way. No person can exist as a purely individual being. A meaningful identity is only possible as part of the extended family or, ultimately, the larger tribal community. The principle of life is: "I am because we are." Surviving as a minority in a threatening environment is only possible in the context of a strong community. This is especially true for those (including believers from a Muslim background) who have lost the support of their own extended family. The Christian community that provides such a community differs, however, from the traditional structures because it is not built on blood-ties and stretches beyond the tribal level.

The challenge of this alternative to a fight and flight approach is to build a vibrant, living and true community that is a meaningful resource and support even in times of oppression and counter forces. God's new society – the term is John Stott's – is called to shine like stars amidst the darkness (Phil 2:15). In Western postmodern societies, this requires different structures than in traditional Eastern cultures, but in every context worship is at the heart of it. God is after all the foundation of this community. Christ has elected himself a bride (Eph 1:4; Rev 19:7), he has rescued and cleansed her through his blood (Eph 5:25-27) and continues to nourish and strengthen her through the power of the Holy Spirit (Rom 15:13). It is this triune God that is honoured in the church. Therefore, I consider worship to be the main feature of the Christian community. Worship can and does, of course, have many different connotations — varying from submitting to God in devotion and obedience to expressing adoration with music and singing. Here I would like to define it as: celebrating the triune God in word and deed.

With seven qualifications I would like to further define the worshipping community in order to show more distinctly what this alternative approach implies. My seven points are adapted from Marva Dawn's book *A Royal Waste of Time*.

A God-centred community

A community with a heart of worship is continuously drawn into God's presence. Since worship is basically celebrating the triune God, it acknowledges God as the centre of life and of the community, and intends to bring people back to God as the centre of life.

An alternative community

The worshipping community should not be considered as an escape from reality – a kind of withdrawal into a pleasant and comfortable community. Neither is it meant as a Christian alternative to Western consumerism. Worship results first of all in a continuous renewal of life, so that this community will reflect God's intentions for creation more and more. Therefore, worship builds an alternative society.

A united community

The alternative character of the worshipping community is primarily expressed in its unity. This unifying quality goes against the grain of both Western and Eastern cultures. The postmodern West is marked by fragmentation; relationships depend on choice and taste, and therefore can change whenever it suits the people involved. In the East, fragmentation is along family or tribal lines. The unity of the Christian community depends not on choice, nor on family ties, nor on blood bonds, but on the unity of the Spirit of Christ. The church that, in worship, continually enters into the presence of God possesses a unity that surpasses family ties and individual choice.

A suffering community.

The worshiping community can only be present in this world as a suffering community. Suffering is not the negation of worship – it is part of it. True worship can only be expressed from a position of suffering, because worship connects the believers with the reality of God and of his love. This love is felt in the pain of suffering for an unfaithful world that has rejected God. Worship connects us with God's pain over a broken creation. Sharing the heart of God implies sharing the cross. The community of Christ suffers with Christ in order to also be glorified with him (Rom 8:17).

An eschatological community

Worship means celebrating the glory of God as it appeared in Christ. However, this is still temporary. The church is the living embodiment of the new life of the *eschaton*, the final restoration of all things, which has already begun. Yet it is aware of the fact that the fullness of the eschaton is still awaiting us. The presence of God in the community is real, yet not completed. Therefore, the Christian community worships God in expectation of the fullness of his glory – when they will see Him face to face. The ultimate *visio Dei* will result in the ultimate worship. Then the whole creation that is groaning will obtain the freedom of the glory of the children of God (Rom 8:21). In the Spirit the church possesses the first fruits of that glory – the first taste of what is to come (Rom 8:23). Therefore, in worship the church anticipates the fullness of the new life.

A wandering community

Because the church is an eschatological community, it is also a wandering community – a nation of pilgrims. They follow Christ and therefore have no place to lay their heads (Luke 9:58). The worshipping community is not characterized by expensive buildings, cathedrals, or by strong church organizations, but by the living fellowship of people that gather for worship. Therefore the Christian community can never disappear, not even when it is too small to fund a church building. Ultimately, even the regulations for *dhimmis* under Islamic rule – although they can put a local community under a lot of pressure – cannot truly threaten the body of Christ, because the essence of the church is not the freedom to repair churches, nor the display of a cross on a building, but the living fellowship of believers. Therefore, there is no need for an armed struggle to preserve those rights; the church does not depend on them. It is the community of two or three people who can come together without any power structures and institutions.

That does not suggest that the church will always be present in all places, but that the presence and the survival of the Christian community cannot be guaranteed by force or power. It also does not suggest that this is easy. It includes suffering.

A missionary community

The worshiping community is always a missionary community; worship is at the heart of mission. For worship brings worshippers close to and into the presence of God, and that in turn will be reflected in their lives. At first sight, mission seems to be impossible for the church with a minority status. However, in the light of what we have just seen, it is the opposite. Even – or especially – as dhimmis, believers can be witnesses, provided that there are enough Christians in one area to constitute at least some kind of community or fellowship. If believers or Muslims who have become followers of Christ have to hide, as in different strict Islamic contexts, the concrete reality might be difficult. Nevertheless, the fact that Christians do not (aspire) to have political power over others is in itself a witness to the character and nature of the Gospel. True mission springs from humble awareness of the presence of God and from the cross of Christ as the core of that presence. Even the smallest, most humble communities of two or three can become places where that divine presence materializes.

Mission is implicit in being a true, vital, and alternative community. That community might be similar ethnically to its environment. Christians do not have to leave their ethnicity, culture and language behind to be Christian. In this way they can continue to relate to family and friends. Very often their resistance to Christianity is the fear of betrayal of the tribal identity and an acceptance of Western culture, politics and power. Once it is clear that God's love incarnates and enters into the world, people are much more open to see how this gospel transforms people within that culture in terms of values, beliefs and ethics. In that the Christian community is also countercultural. Its principles are taken from the gospel of unconditional love. It is expressed by fighting injustice and by looking after everyone in need, not just those of one's own tribe or people. It is living without self-interest and without the motivation to gain politically or economically. It is self-sacrificial. What that looks like in specific circumstances is not a given but needs to be discovered over and over again, by asking to what extent the Christian community resembles and reflects the identity of Christ.

With that, mission has been substantially qualified. Mission in the world of Islam – as in any place – can never be, as the crusaders believed, to repossess what Christendom has lost, but, to use Kenneth Cragg's words, only to restore to Muslims the Christ they never knew.

The Remnant and the Minority Community

An important theme in the Bible is the idea of the "remnant" of the people of God. Especially the Old Testament prophets speak regularly about a remnant of Israel that will be rescued and return to the land (cf. Isa 10:10-22; 37:31; Jer 23:3; Amos 5:15; Mic 2:12; and Gen 45:7) In a similar way Paul speaks about those Jews who like himself believe in Jesus Christ as the "remnant" of Israel (Rom 11:5). Paul assures Israel that God will never break his covenant with his people. The remnant is a sign that not all the believers have become unfaithful and liable of judgment and are therefore a promise for the future. In the end, God is faithful to save – as Paul says – even all Israel (Rom. 11:26).

The idea of the remnant is substantially different from the idea of being a minority. The "remnant" is a concept that is regularly used in a context of unbelief and judgment (cf. Rom 9:27 and 11:4), while being a minority in the context of Islam is not the remnant of a larger group of Christians who have become unfaithful and liable of judgment. Nevertheless, Christ's promise that the gates of hell shall not prevail against the Church is an encouragement for a church that is a vulnerable minority amid a majority of Muslims.

Conclusion

In short, we can define the challenge for the church in the context of Islam, both in the West as in the non-Western world, as building a true worshipping community. This community does not have to fear anything because it does not possess anything in this world that can be taken away from it. It is the community that has taken up the cross to sincerely follow Christ to the end. The members of this community have no guarantee that they will not face suffering or persecution, because it is the mark of the Christian life to suffer with Christ – with or without sharia law. But the promise is that this suffering with Christ is an intrinsic element of the road that leads to glorification with him. In this way, the church is always called to proclaim in word and deed the Kingdom of Christ that is not of this world. Only this type of community will be fruitful, regardless of its numbers.

The Salt of the Earth, the Light of the World

Being a Minority Church in the Context of an Islamic Majority

Petrus Sugito

Introduction

The central idea of this chapter is well expressed in Ephesians 3:17: ". . . so that Christ may dwell in your hearts through faith. And I pray that you, being rooted and established in love, may have power, together with all the Lord's holy people, to grasp how wide and long and high and deep is the love of Christ."

In this chapter I will share reflections and experiences rather than theological thought. What I will share is based on more than fifteen of leadership in the Gereja Kristen Java Tengah Utara (GKJTU), a denomination with around twenty thousand members. This church is one with double minority status. The GKJTU is a part of Christianity in Indonesia, which is a minority religion in a predominantly Islamic society. Furthermore, among the Indonesian denominations, the GKJTU is a small, minority church.

These are my personal thoughts on how to be a minority church within a context of religious plurality with Islam as the majority and the GKJTU vision, mission, strategy, programmes and activities. I hope that the GKJTU as a case study will shed light on how to be a minority church in an Islamic context. I also hope that my contribution will be an inspiration in a process of learning and exchange among GZB's partners.

This chapter is divided in three parts. First, there is a reflection on the concepts of majority and minority. What does the Bible say about the existence of the church as a minority? Secondly, I will present a SWOT analysis (strengths, weaknesses, opportunities and threats) of minority churches in Islamic contexts. Thirdly, I will emphasize that it is necessary for minority churches to be relevant in their mission and ministry. Only when they do so are they the salt of the earth and the light of the world.

Majority and Majority: Sociological and Demographic Terms or More?

The existence of majorities and minorities goes back to the very beginnings of human societies and communities. When Abraham received God's calling to leave for the Promised Land, his group was a minority among nations. When there was a shortage of food in Canaan and he became a refugee in Egypt, Abraham experienced a minority crisis. He was afraid to lose his beautiful wife. He compromised his integrity and he lied to Pharaoh that Sarah was his sister. This was an event related to majority-minority dynamics. My question is whether this is merely a sociological and demographic reality or whether we can take a theological view of this. In other words, are minority-majority dynamics are part of God's plan?

Majority and minority as a sociological reality can be defined as a comparison of communities. The majority is a community with a large number of people, while the minority is a community with a small number of people. Both of them live together in a geographical area. The terms majority and minority are not only about religions but also about racial or ethnic groups. Often there is a relation between religious and ethnic identities. If ethnicity and religion are closely related in a majority community, as is the case in Indonesia, repercussions of the majority-minority dynamics are felt in culture, economics, and politics.

I state the question again for the Indonesian case. In Indonesia, Islam is the majority religion and Christianity the minority religion. Is this just a sociological and demographic reality, or is this an order given by God? The question can also be applied to the specific case of the GKJTU. This small church has the desire to grow in membership. We have made many efforts and implemented various strategies to make the church grow. However, the reality is that we are stagnant as a quantitatively small church. Is there something wrong with the church? Is there something wrong in its vision, its mission, its strategies, its programmes and activities? Is there a flaw on the level of structure and leadership system? Or is its existence as a minority church a divine gift? To be honest, we do not know the answer yet. We hope to find an answer as we exchange experiences with other churches in Muslim majority contexts.

My quest for an answer to the question of whether being a minority or a majority church is God's gift begins with an ecclesiological approach. What is a church? Theologians have given widely diverging definitions of the church. What they all seem to have in common is that a church always has two dimensions. The first dimension is God's dimension. The church cannot be understood without God. It is related to God's saving work in Jesus Christ. The identity of the church is essentially linked to God's plan. The church belongs to God. The second dimension of the church is the human dimension. The existence of the church is the manifestation of the human response to God's work. God entrusted human beings to take a part in managing the church's existence.

These two dimensions are the essence of the church, whether it is part of a minority or part of a majority. The church cannot exist, as majority or minority, without God's permission. For God is the owner, the leader, and the head of the church. And by its very existence, the church can be a means to glorify God.

The terms majority and minority describe the pluralistic context in which churches exist, including a context with different religions. The GKJTU has articulated its views on religious plurality in a supplement to the Heidelberg Catechism, which the GKJTU has adopted as its creedal statement. In recent years, theologians from the GKJTU have written a supplement to the Heidelberg Catechism with reflections on contemporary issues. At the end of this chapter, you will find some relevant paragraphs from the supplement that concern religious plurality.

The Minority Complex of Minorities

What are the strengths, weaknesses, opportunities and threats of a minority church in predominantly Islamic Indonesia? Instead of threats it is perhaps better to speak about challenges to its witness, its diakonia and its fellowship.

The opportunity that Indonesian Islam provides is its relative tolerance compared to, for instance, the form Islam has found in some countries in the Middle East. Coming to the strengths, Christianity in Indonesia generally has a strong social capital. It has a good public image. It enjoys the trust of many. It has a good reputation in the health and education ministries. Some well-known figures and national leaders are graduates of Christian schools. Many people go to Christian hospitals to get health care. In villages, church members usually have a relatively good general knowledge as well as leadership and management skills. For that reason, local communities often trust Christians to be on local committees or to take leadership in organizing local matters. Churches are commonly more responsive and proactive when it comes to humanitarian disasters.

For minorities, the main challenge is a psychological one. The Indonesian historian Azyumardi Azra calls this the "psychology of majority-

minority" in religiously plural societies. According to Azra, this psychological complex emerges, survives and grows in the experience of long
interaction. He also describes the anxiety in a religious community when
it comes to face-to-face with other religious groups.

In this context, conflict and violence between different religious
communities occur. They arise from a consciousness based on the collective memory of each religious community. A collective memory is not
easily erased. Indeed, it can surface at any time and it may manifest itself
in forms of large-scale communal violence triggered by small conflicts. A
minority often harbours anxiety or fear in the face of a majority surrounding them. It fears not only for its position in society but for its very
existence, to which the majority poses a threat.

A common and nearly irrepressible fear of religious minorities in
Muslim majority contexts is the myth of the Islamic nation. In dialogue
meetings, I have often come across this fear. It boils down to this: religious minorities believe that Muslims in Indonesia want to establish an
Islamic nation by means of a peaceful evolution and by violent means
such as the rebellion of Darul Islam. I believe such feelings are part of a
psychological minority complex. They are irrational and entrench minority structures in Indonesia. As a result, the existential struggle within the
religious minorities intensifies.

In the last two decades, the existential fear of religious minorities has
grown in reaction to the so-called *santrinisasi*. This is a movement that
promotes enrolment in Islamic education in boarding schools. Minorities
have perceived this movement as a threat to their existence.

The Minority Complex of the Majority

The psychological minority complex of exaggerated fear is mirrored by a
psychological minority complex inside the Islamic majority in Indonesia.
This too is a result of complex historical, sociological, and political factors. In the 1980s, the Dutch sociologist C.A.O. van Nieuwenhuijze described Indonesian Islam as a "majority with a minority complex". What
he meant was that the majority had the attitude of a minority. This is
rooted, of course, in the Indonesian experience of colonialism. Muslims
experienced marginalization on a social, economic and political level.
This sense of marginalization continued during the reigns of Sukarno and
Suharto, respectively called the Old Order and New Order, during which
Muslim political parties, organizations and Muslim representatives
(*santri*) felt side-lined. Hence, the religious majority had a minority com-

plex: Muslims felt isolated in their own land by their own government, which they did not really consider as their government.

This minority complex of Indonesian Islam has exacerbated fears toward other religious minorities, especially Christians. Many Muslims have perceived Christians as a group with an aggressive agenda to conquer Indonesia through a program of Christianization. In their eyes, Christianization is conducted in various ways, not only by persuasive evangelism, but also by enticing Muslims to become Christians with financial support for education, health, or food, thus exploiting the poverty of Muslims.

These stereotypes have captured the imagination of many Muslims. They view Christian minorities as aggressive and expansionist, from the colonial era up to the present. Whereas Christianization used to be supported by the Netherlands, it is now believed to rely on funding from churches worldwide, particularly from the United States. American churches are not only known for their strong financial resources and enthusiastic evangelists, but also for their courage in taking dramatic evangelistic steps.

Based on these premises, the "majority with a minority complex" has created a conspiracy theory. Muslims believe that there is a conspiracy in Western Christianity to destroy Islam and convert all Muslims to Christianity. Part of the perceived conspiracy is the conquest of Muslim areas, as was carried out by Europe between the eighteenth century and World War II.

Religious Freedom in Indonesia

The space for Indonesian churches appears to be narrowing, with many more Muslims wishing to implement sharia legislation in various aspects of life. The editorial of the daily *Kompas* of 5 March 2008 reviewed research conducted in five large universities in Indonesia (UI, ITB, UGM, University of Airlangga and Brawijaya). The outcome of this research indicated that 80 percent of the students would prefer sharia law over the *Pancasila* as the foundation of the Indonesian state. The *Pancasila* is the doctrine that became the official philosophy of independent Indonesia and safeguarded religious freedom. Indonesia's first president, Sukarno, introduced the *Pancasila* in 1945. It comprises five principles: belief in God, nationalism, humanitarianism, social justice and democracy. Ever since 1945 conservative Islamic leaders have expressed their concern that Islam was not given a more prominent and special role in Indonesia's constitution. As this research illustrates, in recent years the number of people who share this concern has grown.

Today, religious freedom is limited and the government is unable to prevent violence in the name of religion. A report of the SETARA Institute, an NGO that concerns itself with religious freedom, counted 244 violations of this freedom in the year 2011. Another recent study on religious radicalisation among students shows alarming data. It was carried out by the NGO LaKIP in Jakarta over the months October 2010 to January 2011. The *Koran Tempo* (25 April 2011) reported its outcomes as follows.

			Student	Teacher
1	Are you willing to carry out violence in the name of religion?	=	48,9%	28,2%
2	Are you willing to damage facilities belonging to other religions?	=	41,1%	22,7%
3	Do you agree with the enforcement of Islamic sharia?	=	84,8%	76,2%
4	Is the *Pancasila* irrelevant as the basis of the state?	=	25,8%	21,1%

The Strengths of a Religious Minority

What are the strengths of religious minorities? Minorities are often characterised by solid identities and high solidarity. A minority is therefore easier to manage and problems inside the group are more easily solved.

The Indonesian theologian Eka Darmaputera (1942-2005) said that minority groups tend to be more creative and innovative. He used the analogy of a small aircraft, such as the F-16, with which a pilot can manoeuvre with more ease and speed. A majority is like a large aircraft such as a Jumbo Jet, a Boeing, or an Airbus, with hundreds of passengers. It is much harder for a pilot to manoeuvre such large airplanes than the small ones.

Weaknesses are often the flip side of strengths, and minorities are often politically marginalized. They have less economic power than the majorities. Minorities have limited human resources. As I explained above, minorities often experience minority complexes.

The Mission of a Minority Church

Regardless of the strengths, weaknesses, opportunities and threats, the church must be church in a context of Islamic majorities. What does it take for the church as a minority to be relevant and to be reckoned with by the majority? The answer to that question is easy to give, but not easy to implement. To be relevant, the church should be the real salt and light of the world. What does the GKJTU do to be the salt and the light? We have developed an integral teaching on mission that involves each member of our church. At the heart of our view of mission are the following notions.

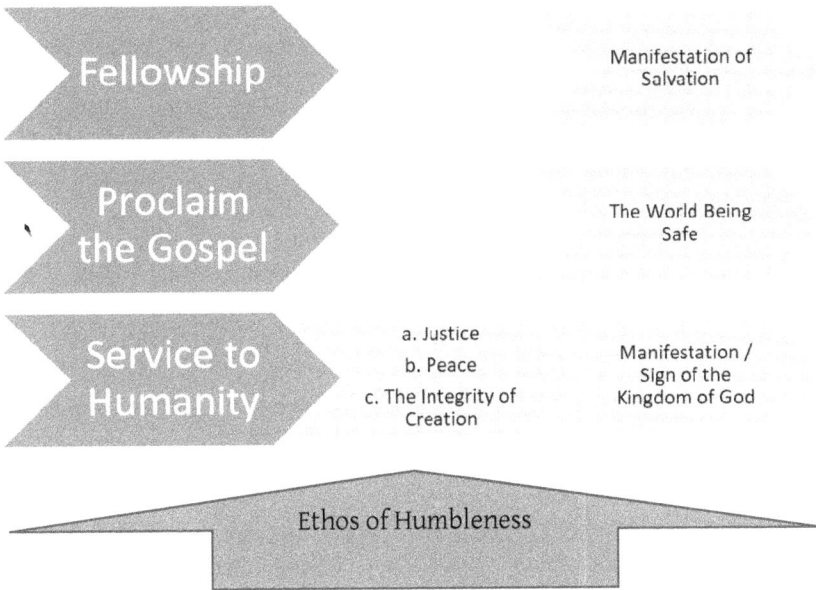

Fellowship

Manifestation of
Salvation

Proclaim
the Gospel

The World Being
Safe

Service to
Humanity

a. Justice

b. Peace

c. The Integrity of
Creation

Manifestation /
Sign of the
Kingdom of God

Ethos of Humbleness

This missions diagram may be explained as follows: The GKJTU as a church has a mission, a calling, a duty in the world and for the world. The whole and comprehensive mission of the GKJTU is to help realize God's salvation in this world, both individually and socially, spiritually and materially. The implementation of that mission can be broken down into three main callings or duties: a mission of community (fellowship), a mission of evangelization (testimony) and a mission of service to humanity (diakonia).

These three callings need further clarification. Fellowship is formed to receive salvation from Jesus Christ. It is also the foundation and starting point of the community of the believers. Evangelization is the mandate given by Jesus Christ to share the good news. God's salvation in the name of Jesus is aimed at saving the world. This is the purpose of the church's testimony. Service to humanity, also called diakonia, intends to bring God's love to the world. It encompasses what I call the creation mission, salvation mission, and reconciliation mission. The creation mission is the protection and preservation of all creation. Human behaviour has resulted in a broken and bruised world. The church seeks to restore creation, so that it may become the new creation. The salvation mission sets people free from the handcuffs of sufferings, injustice, oppression, etc. The reconciliation mission, or peaceful mission, is done by God for human beings in Jesus Christ. In a world that is full of conflicts, the church is called to help reconcile people who are in conflict.

The church must carry out all these forms of mission out of selfless and honest service. In its mission, the church observes the servant ethos that Jesus Christ exemplified. It does its mission as a servant works for their employer.

In the diagram, the church's three duties, the fellowship mission, evangelization mission and humanity mission, have been indicated by parallel arrows. This signifies that the three forms of mission cannot be separated. They must keep pace with one another. One form of mission cannot be elevated over another, nor can another form of mission be ignored. All three must be done together, reinforcing one another.

Channels of God's Blessing

How do we implement integral mission teaching? In the GKJTU, we are active, creative and innovative in social work. We want to help in overcoming social problems in order to be a channel of blessing for people from different backgrounds. We also actively pray for the majority and for the welfare of all. We are inspired by the words of Psalm 122:6-7: "Pray for the peace of Jerusalem: 'May those who love you be secure. May there be peace within your walls and security within your citadels,'" and by the words of Jeremiah 29:7: "Also, seek the peace and prosperity of the city to which I have carried you into exile. Pray to the Lord for it, because if it prospers, you too will prosper."

In a pluralistic context, we try to be a channel of the Lord's blessing for others. This is an important element of the vision of the GKJTU. We also wish to grow in our ability to be such channels of blessing. We wish to make the GKJTU more meaningful. To that end, we are trying to go beyond the charitable diaconal paradigm to a transformative diaconal paradigm. Practically, that means that we are involved in the following initiatives: (1) organic farming to help overcome the environmental crisis; (2) introducing renewable energy to help overcome the energy crisis; (3) developing credit unions to help overcome the economic crisis; (4) fostering character formation to help overcome the character crisis; (5) offering counselling to help people overcome psychological crises and unhealthy lifestyles; (6) participating in interfaith dialogue to help relieve the tensions between the faith communities and (7) raising awareness to help minimize the risk of natural disasters and providing aid to its victims.

In addition to the general strategy described above, we promote values such as self-reliance, integrity, team work, transparency, accuracy, and professionalism. The leadership styles we try to develop are servant leadership (Mark 10:43-45), collective leadership and team work.

Inclusive Mission, Exclusive Identity

In its organization, the GKJTU as a minority church relies first of all on spiritual, social, and human resources. Secondly, it needs physical and financial sources. Spiritual capital starts with a strong belief in one's values, which is followed by a personal commitment, and finally a collective commitment. Social capital is an ability to cooperate with each other based on mutual trust to achieve common goals. The strength of our social and spiritual capital will enable us to gain both sensitivity and empathy (2 Cor 2: 3-5).

A minority group must be inclusive in its mission, but exclusive in its identity. The identity should be strong, as the New Testament emphasizes in different ways. "Therefore, my dear brothers and sisters, stand firm. Let nothing move you. Always give yourselves fully to the work of the Lord, because you know that your labour in the Lord is not in vain." (1 Cor 15:58) ". . . so that Christ may dwell in your hearts through faith. And I pray that you, being rooted and established in love, may have power, together with all the Lord's holy people, to grasp how wide and long and high and deep is the love of Christ." (Eph 3:17)

Our strategy to bolster the identity of our church is characterized by the following terms: reaffirming, strengthening, and manifesting the church's Reformed identity. Our identity is reinforced when we grow in a spirituality and ethics based on the Bible, the Heidelberg Catechism, and the Supplement to the Heidelberg Catechism that we have adopted as a creedal statement.

The church remains the church, be it in a minority or a majority context. The church should be the salt of the earth and the light of the world. The difference between a majority and a minority church is not in their substance, but in their strategies to be that salt and light. Especially relevant to minority churches are Jesus' words: "I am sending you out like sheep among wolves. Therefore be as shrewd as snakes and as innocent as doves." (Matt 10:16)

Excerpts from the GKJTU's Supplement to the Heidelberg Catechism

Question: What is meant by "plurality" and "pluralism"?

Answer: "Plurality" denotes the variety found in reality. In Indonesia, a huge variety of ethnic groups, colours of skin, religions, languages etc. can be found. "Pluralism" is a view or attitude concerning this variety. The GKJTU embraces pluralism as a means to accept and appreciate diversity. The plurality found in Indonesia, especially in the different religions, desperately needs pluralism to facilitate living together in mutual respect. This plurality is a challenge permitted by God so that the faith of the believers might be constantly tested.

Question: What is our attitude towards the plurality of religions?

Answer: *Firstly,* the variety of religions is a concrete reality and universal phenomenon. Christians cannot close their eyes to this reality. The church is required to comprehend, be aware of and struggle with this reality, so that it can take the right attitude in the midst of that variety.

Secondly the church respects other religions, but does not regard all religions as equal. Every religion is unique ... Christian faith holds the view that no religion whatsoever can save people. People can only be saved by the initiative of God, not by human efforts or merits ... Christian faith stresses that salvation can only be obtained by life and death of/with Jesus Christ. Those who die outside of Christ and outside the fellowship of the believers can only be left to the authority and sovereignty of God.

Question: In encounters between different religious communities, some take a fanatical attitude by humiliating or even insulting others. One example is to call the adherents of other religions "heathens". What is our attitude when we are called heathens?

Answer: The dictionary of the Indonesian language *Kamus Besar Bahasa Indonesia* explains that *kafir* ("pagan", "heathen") is someone who does not believe in God or in his prophet(s). Therefore the term *kafir* is often used to humiliate or even curse others whose conduct is not according to God's truth, or even for those of a different religion or conviction. But assuming the abovementioned basic meaning of the term, the adherents of other religions must not be called *kafir*, including the Christians. Christian faith very obviously stresses faith in God, who has worked and taken visible form in Jesus Christ. Christians also believe the prophets and apostles, who in a special way have received revelations from God ... Only atheists (people who deny the existence of God) with demeaning behaviour are properly called *kafir*.

When Christians encounter adherents of other religions who call Christians *kafir*, the Christians must not respond in the same way by calling those adherents of other religions *kafir*. The Christian faith does not teach us to repay evil with evil ...

Question: In a situation of religious plurality the religious communities spread their respective religions. This can lead to conflicts among the religious communities. How does the church proclaim the Gospel in the midst of this religious plurality?

Answer: Basically, every religious community has the right to spread its respective religion. Every Christian has the task to proclaim the Gospel, the good news of salvation. Therefore evangelization is not just making somebody change his religion. Evangelization means scattering the seed of the gospel by erecting the signs of the kingdom of God. Therefore the gospel is an offer, not a constraint. Thus evangelization has to be carried out wisely and politely in respect towards the other religious communities ...

Question: How do Christians work out their relationship with other religious communities?

Answer: The individual Christian and the church as a whole have to be open for dialogue and for cooperation with other religious communities. This dialogue will run well if both sides meet in an atmosphere of trust and mutual respect. What should properly be discussed in this dialogue? *Firstly,* there should be a dialogue on the life styles and the right to exist of the respective religious communities. This is very important to create an attitude of mutual respect and cooperation, so that a pattern of positive coexistence can emerge. *Secondly,* there should be a dialogue about the ethics of life in order to create coexistence in dignity. Based on these two principles all religious communities can cooperate.

Question: A society with religious plurality very easily leads to religious intermarriage. What is our view and attitude concerning this issue?

Answer: Indonesian Marriage Laws (no. 1 of the year 1974) decree that a marriage is legal according to the laws of religion. That means that a marriage is legal with civil effects if it is legal according to the laws of the respective religion. As a consequence this decree forbids religious intermarriage. Nevertheless, religious intermarriage is a reality which cannot be denied in the midst of a reality of religious plurality. There are quite a lot of examples of religious intermarriage which were finally resolved by a court decision. So religious intermarriage can be legalized as these precedents of jurisprudence show. But before Christians decide on religious intermarriage they should consider the following: *Firstly,* is the decision to engage in an interreligious marriage really responsible in creating a harmonious family life? *Secondly,* will the decision for religious intermarriage not have negative impacts in the future? Above all it should be kept in mind that God's ideal is a couple of common faith. Therefore every believer is called to bring his family to Christian faith.

Question: It happens that adherents of different religions meet and pray together for the issues they face together. What is our view and attitude concerning these phenomena?

Answer: In every religion people pray as a means to sustain the relationship of their religious community with God. As they face common problems, it can easily happen that people pray together although they belong to different religious communities. Christian faith, and respectively the church, does not forbid its members from attending such interreligious prayers. Nevertheless Christians have to preserve their Christian identity during such prayers, because Christian prayers have their own characteristic. If the prayer is led by a non-Christian, the Christians say their own silent Christian prayer. But if in certain circumstances Christians are asked to lead the prayer they should say a Christian prayer and give the opportunity to adherents of other religions present to say a silent prayer according to their religious conviction. Thus the Christians can show their solidarity with other people through their prayers.

Suffering that Brings Blessing

The Protestants of Luwu, Sulawesi

Lambang Mandi Tandi Pare and Petrus Sugito

This case study shows how the suffering of one generation may bring blessing for a next generation. Fifty years ago, a community of Christians became internally displaced due to violence. The children of this community developed resilience and creativity, with which they blessed their environment and, eventually, their area of origin. In retrospect, they are able to see that the tragedy of the displacement was part of God's good plan, just like in the story of Joseph.

Introduction

Eli Pattudju and his wife Mariana were two of the thousands of victims of the persecution of Christians on Sulawesi in the 1950s and 1960s. They married in 1963. Now Eli Pattudju is on retirement from government employment; his wife is also retired. They have three children, Mery Pattudju, Elman Pattudju, and Arlin Pattudju, and four grandchildren. The oldest child is a pastor in the Indonesian Protestant Chuch of Luwu (GPIL). One of their grandchildren is studying to become a medical doctor. This family had to flee their village because they were Christians. They found refuge in another area and built a new life there.

Like them, many other Christians were forced to seek refuge elsewhere. They were scattered to different places in Sulawesi. Gradually, these places of refuge became Christian villages. Many of the Christians from these villages were quite successful in life. Some of them returned to their original villages to build churches. They forged new relationships with their family members who are Muslim.

The saying is true that Christianity spreads when it is struck down. The family of Eli Pattudju is an example. They started their new life as survivors of sad events; they ended with blessing. The persecution that forced them to move happened a long time ago. But to them it feels like it happened yesterday. They told us their story when we interviewed them in Palopo South Sulawesi, in the month of August 2014.

Christians in the Time of Muzakkar's Uprising

In 1921 Abdul Kahar Muzakkar started a political movement to establish an Islamic state in South Sulawesi, including Palopo. Palopo is the ministry area of the GPIL. This movement ended when Muzakkar was killed by the Indonesian Armed Forces on 3 February 1965. Muzakkar's movement wanted to provide an alternative ideology for Indonesia after its independence. Muzakkar offered an Islamic system, which favoured the Islamic majority. In fact, he wanted to turn Indonesia into an independent Islamic state. Muzakkar joined forces with indigenous armed groups that were fighting for independence. After Indonesia became independent, Muzakkar's forces were automatically incorporated into the Indonesian army. In 1952, however, as a reaction to the policy of the national army in Jakarta, he established an armed wing of his political movement. His militia was called the *Tentara Keamanan Rakyat* or People's Security Army in South Sulawesi.

At that time, the Islamic mystic and guerrilla leader Sekarmadji Maridjan Kartasuwirjo led a rebellion in West Java and formed the *Darul Islam* or Islamic State. The Darul Islam also had an armed wing, the Islamic Army of Indonesia. Muzakkar got in contact with Kartasuwirjo. After negotiations, they agreed to merge their armies. On 7 August 1953 Muzakkar declared his desertion from the Indonesian National Army. He declared himself an enemy of the secular state in Indonesia and announced his wish to make Indonesia an Islamic state. For approximately fifteen years Muzakkar and his troops, young people recruited from the villages in South Sulawesi, conducted a guerrilla war in the hinterlands of South, Southeast, and Central Sulawesi.

In the areas affected by Muzakkar's guerrillas, there were many small Christian communities, who lived there as minority groups. These Christian groups were maltreated by the rebel groups. The guerrillas forced many Christians to change their faith at gunpoint and become Muslims. They also violently forced them to support their movement to build an Indonesian Islamic state. Many were murdered because of their unwavering faithfulness to Christ.

Many Christians chose to leave their villages and go to the city of Palopo. Palopo and its surroundings became a safe haven for them. The government set up some refugee camps around Palopo city. People who chose to stay in these camps had to work day and night to start new lives in their new surroundings. They lost their properties in their villages. They separated from their relatives because they had a different faith. It was a deep human tragedy.

A Creative Minority of Refugees

These tragic events happened fifty years ago. Today most of the victims have a new perspective on what happened back then. They continued to send their children to school and they continued to practise their faith. They built and planted new churches. In the refugee camps, they struggled to stay faithful. They had to fight for their survival. They had to be faithful to God in a new place.

Eli Pattudju told us that, during the most difficult days of the persecution, he decided to convert to Islam. In 1954, he moved to Seriti, one of the assigned places of refuge, to start a new life. In this place, he converted back to Christianity. Eli was not the only one who did this.

In the refugee camp the Christians became a creative minority. The challenges and hardships they faced forced them to become hard workers and to mature in faith. Today, these refugee camps are Christian villages. In general, these villages are more prosperous than others. The children have a higher level of education than in other villages.

The refugees built new relationships with their original village. They were able to support construction projects in their villages. In the context of the GPIL, we discovered that the founders of this church are first and second generation victims of Muzakkar. Similarly, most the church members are first, second, and third generation victims of the guerrillas. Most of the pastors in this church are second and third generation survivors too.

Turning Evil to Good

We reflected theologically. Our reflection was based on Genesis 50:20 "You intended to harm me, but God intended it for good to accomplish what is now being done, the saving of many lives." Fifty years ago, Muzakkar intended to harm the believers, but God intended it for good, to accomplish what is being done now.

We observed that the relations between Muslims and Christians in the land of Luwu remained good and peaceful over a long period of time. The foundations for these peaceful relations were laid in the original villages of the former refugees. The former refugees brought reconciliation, because they remained connected to the extended family system. Some from the younger generation became the channel of the Lord's blessing to their home villages. They gave financial support or expertise that helped build and improve their villages.

The Christian communities in the refugee camps did not disappear. In the case of GPIL, many of these communities became self-reliant congregations. Data about GPIL congregations in the Palopo area demonstrate the impact of the victims of Muzakkar. In and around the village of Seriti there are three congregations with a total of one hundred-twenty member families. Around the villages of Lamasi and Pongsamelung there are two congregations with a total of one hundred-seventy member families. The area of the Lalong village counts four congregations made up of two hundred families in all. In the area of Rantai Damai there are two congregations with one hundred families. In the Tabah village there is one congregation with forty-two member families.

This is the way God develops the church and takes it from somewhere to everywhere. God took the intention of a human being to harm believers and turned it into something good, to accomplish what is being done today.

The Blessing of Overcoming Fear

The Remarkable Growth of Algerian Churches in Recent Years

Youssef Yacob

This chapter tells the story of the remarkable growth of Evangelical churches in Algeria in recent years. It points out that it was only after young Christians overcame their fear that the churches started growing. In spite of the horrors of the civil war (1992-2002) and a temporary restriction of religious freedom and a crackdown on the churches (2006-2011), Christianity has spread to most Algerian villages, towns and cities.

The Seed Planted

A quick review of Algeria's church and mission history teaches us that the Protestant missionaries who came to the country in 1881 were very faithful. Some of them stayed for more than forty years. They made great sacrifices. The results of their work may seem meagre, but they managed to plant seeds in the hearts and lives of many. At the time of these missionaries, Algeria was colonised by the French. As a result, Algerians were not open to the gospel, as they linked it to colonialism and oppression. In 1961, when Algeria became independent and more missionaries came to the country, the missionaries managed to establish a church in Algiers and a small group in the Western city of Oran. This group was fragile and struggled. There were other Christians, but they were scattered around the country.

Initially, there was no Christian church among the mountainous Kabyle. This changed when, according to God's amazing plan, the believers from Oran and Algiers organized an evangelistic camp in the Kabyle area. They encountered many young people who came to play football in a tournament. The Christians camped with them and tried to find ways to evangelize and share the gospel with them. The Lord gave them wisdom and they managed to establish contact. They prayed for a sick young man who later came to faith.

From the forty young people who came to faith many abandoned Christianity and returned to Islam. The authorities were still persecuting

Christians with a background in Islam. It was a difficult time for new believers. Many missionaries were expelled and their churches were shut
down. It was difficult for the believers to find ways to meet and to have
fellowship.

Four Young Preachers

Only four young men, who had decided to follow Jesus at any cost, were
led by the Spirit to meet. The Lord began to bless them and work through
them. Despite their lack of training and pastoral care, the Holy Spirit was
truly in their midst. Amazingly, this early church in the Kabyle area,
which started in the 1980s, decided to fast for one year, seek the Lord,
and meditate in the mountains. In the second year, they continued fasting for nine more months. Then the Holy Spirit came upon them in a very
powerful way, in unexplainable measures. The Lord helped them to overcome their fear of people and channel this fear into the fear of God. Because they overcame their fear, they continued to meet. They took courage from many Scripture passages about fear and trusting the Lord's
power, his presence, and the manifestation of the Holy Spirit.

The four went out to preach in different villages, in universities in the
Kabyle area, and in an electronics company with between four and five
thousand workers. The students and workers came from different villages and towns in the Kabyle region. Once they were touched by the gospel,
they returned to their friends and family and began to spread the word.
By the late 1980s, the church was becoming well established in the area.
Not only were the believers experiencing the powerful presence of the
Holy Spirit, but they were also overcoming their fear. They began to witness openly by visiting people, sharing with them and experiencing wonderful things happening in their midst.

Church Growth During and After the Civil War

Between 1992 and 2002 a civil war raged in Algeria. Islamists were
fighting against the Algerian government, attempting to establish an Islamic state. These were some of the darkest years in Algeria's history.
The Muslim fundamentalists killed many people, and amongst them were
some Christians; many others were truly protected by the Lord. The Roman Catholic Church lost nineteen people, some of whom were bishops,
nuns, and priests.

At that time, many people thought that the church in Algeria was
vanishing, as the believers were scattered and tempted to flee. In spite of

that, they continued to fast, seek God, and experience the presence and protection of the Holy Spirit. The church entered into a deeper relationship and fellowship with the Lord Jesus. Because of the civil war, Algerians began to ask questions about Islam. How could all of these crimes be committed in the name of Islam? Many became open to other ideas and religions and responded to the gospel. Christian TV and radio channels were instrumental in communicating the gospel. Many believers decided to proclaim the good news on the TV channels by sharing their stories and testimonies. The stories did not only come from abroad: believers from Algeria also shared their stories. Many Algerian people heard this and became very receptive to the Christian message.

When we look back on the time between 1981 and 2015, the Lord has brought an incredible change in Algeria, especially in Kabyle. Today there are Christians in almost every village or town. In each of the almost 2,400 towns and villages across the country there is a Christian presence. We estimate that tens of thousands of people have come to faith. Thousands get baptized each year. Communities range from small groups of believers who meet in their homes to a church of eleven hundred members that gathers every weekend to worship and pray. In the midst of this incredible growth, people have become very bold in their outreach: they share with no fear.

Religious Freedom Restricted

Many Arab governments and Islamic Associations have pressured the Algerian government to clamp down on the churches to stop their growth and to prevent more Muslims from leaving Islam and becoming Christians. Because of this pressure, the Algerian government took the position that there is another danger besides terrorism: the appeal of Christianity.

In March 2006, the Algerian parliament passed Ordinance 06-03, which seriously restricted religious liberty. The alleged aim of this ordinance was to organize non-Muslim worship; the real objective was to restrict Christians, frighten the believers, and close down the churches. One of the articles in the new law stated that "you are not allowed to meet in any building which is not meant for religious purposes". Due to this new law, most of the churches had to close down, as most of the Christians met in garages or homes. In addition, the article also states that "if you shake the faith of Muslims, either by sharing with them your faith by giving them something to read or by even giving them something good, you will be in trouble". Consequently, church leaders can be given prison sentences of one to five years and fines amounting to 14,000 dollars. Church membership may lead to one to three years in prison and a fine of up to 7,000 dollars. The ordinance also stated that it is against the law to travel with Christian books or to keep them in one's home. The new law was implemented in the years 2007 and 2008. Magistrates ordered twenty-six churches to close down because the authorities claimed that they were meeting in homes and buildings that were not meant for religious purposes.

The Algerian government did not realize that God had helped the Algerian church to overcome fear in an amazing way. Despite the laws and consequences set in place, the Algerian Christians continued to meet at any cost. They accepted the new position they were in, but they did not give up. After the orders expressed by the authorities, only one church actually closed down, but even that was due to family problems. Because of our evangelistic activities, we have had ongoing court cases. One of our team members has been to court nine times because of participating in evangelistic activities and being caught travelling with Christian books.

In a paradoxical way, this law became a great blessing to the church. It was discussed in various newspapers and magazines. Even though many authors wrote negatively about the church and falsely accused it, God has used them to spread the word of Algerian Christians and their courage in continuing their fellowship throughout the country. We have had many opportunities to witness within the courts and police stations. In every situation God has chosen to work in every single believer. This has led people to sympathize with the church and with Christians. In spite of the law, we have gained support in many ways. Support also came from Christians around the world who were praying and from Western governments that pressured the Algerian government. The years 2007 and 2008 were a fierce battle, but God enabled the believers of Algeria to stand firm with no fear of people, but only fear of God and his words.

"The Biggest Miracle I Have Ever Seen"

After these years of persecution, on 17 July 2011 the Algerian government decided to give us an official license. This license allowed Christians to freely meet in their church buildings, to register local church communities, to register our workers within the social security system and so on. I believe that this was the biggest miracle that I have ever seen in my life. The Islamic government fully recognized a church from a Muslim background. As far as I know, Algeria is the first country to make these ad-justments.

This incredible breakthrough allowed us to see how God had blessed the young people when they decided to overcome fear and proclaimed the word of God by depending on the Holy Spirit through prayer and fast-ing. From that little group in 1981 the church has evolved and has be-come a well-established and very significant community in most areas of Algeria. The church continues to grow, especially in the city of Oran and the Kabyle area.

I am deeply convinced that when believers in other parts of the world decide to stand firm for the sake of the gospel and for the sake of Jesus, God will manifest himself in special ways. The church and its believers will experience great blessings as they decide to overcome fear and put their trust in the Lord and his protection. In addition, I believe that per-fect love casts out fear. When we decide to love the Lord Jesus and spend time with him in fellowship, in reading his words and fasting, our rela-tionship with him deepens. By trusting him at any price, God hands us the wisdom and the boldness to share our faith with love and humility.

Three Encouraging Stories

In Algeria, some examples have been a great blessing to all Christians. A Christian couple from the Western part of the country had a baby girl. They decided to call her Esther. When they went to register her at the town hall, the clerks refused to do so. Her name was a non-Muslim name, they said. They were not allowed to call their girl Esther. The father stood his ground and insisted on the name Esther. He explained that he and his wife were Christians and that they wished to name their daughter in this way. The clerks then suggested submitting their request to a judge. The judge was the only one who could officially decline or accept the name. So the father went to see the judge and fearlessly presented his case. Once again, he explained that they were Christians and that they wished to call their daughter Esther. The judge requested the baptism certifi-cates of both wife and husband. He initiated a police investigation to see whether the couple were truly Christians. Finally, eighteen months later, having thoroughly checked the background of the couple and their con-stant perseverance, the judge decided in their favour. The judge had come across an article in Algerian law which states: "If the parents are Christians, they are allowed to give their children Christian names". When he came back to the town hall and announced the judgement, the employees were shocked. Even the town hall clerks had not yet heard of this article in civil law. After setting their disbelief aside, they agreed to register the daughter's name as Esther. This couple were converts from Islam. They proclaimed their faith and stood firm in what they believed. Eventually they won the case, not only for themselves, but for many families within the Christian community in Algeria. This step of faith has been a great blessing for not only this family, but for all of us. It showed us that when you stand firm and overcome fear, God will bless.

The second encouraging story is about a young man who has boldly shared the gospel. God has truly motivated many young men and women to be totally devoted to the Lord Jesus. Because of their strong faith in the word of God, they proclaim the gospel with no fear. One of them was this young man, whose court case is presently frozen. After being sentenced to five years imprisonment, he continued to display amazing boldness. He travelled to the West of Algeria, to an area that is very different from the Kabyle region, where he proclaimed the gospel to people on the streets. One day the police caught him after someone had complained about him. When he was caught and arrested, they took him to a small police station. Later he was transferred to a bigger police station, yet he was still not shaken. He managed to witness to sixteen policemen about his personal story. He spoke about the love of God, which touched him so triumphantly, and granted him the wisdom to share. Even after he had been put in prison, he continued to share and speak about his faith. The policemen tried to move him to an isolated cell, away from others, so that he would stop witnessing, but he opened the window and continued to talk about his faith. This brother, who stood up for the Lord Jesus and for his faith, gave tremendous courage to many people in Algeria.

The final story is about a community called the House of Refuge. This is a place where people who suffer for their faith can stay. The three families who live there are completely isolated. The Muslims in their village are fanatics. In spite of that, they live a life devoted to prayer, fasting and connection with the Lord Jesus. With the local mosque only fifty metres away, they are fearless in making themselves known. Shining for God in a risky village where anything can happen, they continue to live by faith, trusting the Lord and living for his gospel. The sheikh of the village, a Quran teacher, is their immediate neighbour. He favours them because he has received love and care from them and he has experienced their uniqueness. He is a man of authority in the village, and yet he is like a family friend to the House of Refuge. His trust in the families at the House of Refuge is so great that he tells people to turn to them whenever he is away. Because he is a sheikh, his trust in the Christians has great symbolical value. The Christians gained his confidence when they chose to overcome fear and allow the Lord to work in them and through them. One of the village teachers mentioned that when the Christian families came to the village, they brought a certain light with them that lit up the village. Like this village, many Muslim communities are hungry and thirsty to see the reality of God in the lives of Christians and to understand who Christians truly are, as opposed to the false teachings they are taught. It is a blessing to see what the Lord does when the church and its believers overcome fear and trust God. This small Christian community of the House of Refuge trusts God's promise and his words. God seems to be at work in the lives of many people in that village.

Finally, the Algerian church needs constant prayer as it seeks to follow and worship God, so that God may help us, by his grace, to never trust in ourselves but put our trust in the Lord Jesus, his word, and his promises. Our heart's desire is to see God's work in Algeria become a great blessing, not only for Algerians, but also on an international level. May God make us good examples to the Arab and Muslim world.

Overcoming Modern Gnosticism

The Evangelical Churches in Egypt

Sameh Ibrahim

The Egyptian Christians live as a minority in an Islamic culture; the vast majority of Egypt's citizens are Muslims. Also, as Evangelical Christians, we live as a minority among a majority of Orthodox Christians. So we have two facts here: we live as religious minority and as a denominational minority. Being a numerical minority is in itself not a problem, but the Christians of Egypt are politically and socially also a relatively weak group. Its weakness often prevents it from being a minority that is fruitful in Egyptian society.

In this chapter, I will discuss the reasons of the socio-political weakness of the Christian minority in Egypt. In my view, two factors erode the position of Christians: the politics of the country and the attitude of the church. Before I come to those issues, I will first give a brief impression of the traumatic experience my community had in 2013.

Churches on Fire

I am the pastor of the Gad el-Seed Evangelical Church in el-Minia in the South of Egypt. El-Minia is a town with a Muslim majority and a Christian minority. Among the Christians of el-Minia Evangelicals represent the minority; Orthodox Christians are the majority. So my church is a minority within the minority.

Our church was the first church in el-Minia to be burnt by terrorists on 14 August 2013. The torching of the church occurred after the ousting of President Muhammad Morsi and the fall of his Islamic government. The Muslim Brotherhood had been democratically elected after the revolution in 2012, but had gradually introduced a number of anti-democratic measures. Christians and Muslims alike joined mass protests against Morsi's government that were triggered by the government's attempt to change the constitution. On 30 June 2013, the large-scale demonstrations began and along with the young people of my church I also participated in these peaceful demonstrations. Eventually, after General Abdel Fattah el-Sisi had unseated Morsi and ended the mass protests, radical Muslims punished their political opponents, among whom they counted the Christians. Sadly, they chose our church as one of their targets.

Paradoxically, it was only during these trying events that we discovered that as Evangelicals we are important to our neighbours. This was clear in the help we received from our Muslim, Orthodox and Catholic fellow citizens, who helped us extinguish the fire inside the church. We have always striven for good relationships between the members of our church and the people living in our area. In our moment of need, they were there to help us.

We have always fostered good relationships with Muslims and Christians of other denominations by our participation in community events such as feasts and our peaceful presence with them in good times and in bad times. When misfortune befell us, the other Christian denominations helped us because we have common ground and Muslim neighbours helped us because we have peaceful relations with them.

A Religious Minority as a Political Threat

As I pointed out, the Muslim Brotherhood terrorists punished the Christians by burning many churches and many buildings belonging to Christians. In my view, this punishment had a political rather than a religious nature. In this case, the Muslim Brotherhood viewed the Christians as a political party.

In Egypt there is no tradition of strong, independent political parties. In other words, we have no clear, effective, political voices that can be critical of the ruling party. That is why during the revolution against Morsi's government the ruling party treated the whole Christian community as its political opponent. Although many different parties joined in the demonstrations against the Freedom and Justice Party, as the Muslim Brotherhood called its political wing, the Muslim terrorists singled out only the Christians, especially in el-Minia. They made the Christians the political enemy of the Muslim Brotherhood.

This type of confusion of religion and politics always creates problematic and dangerous situations. In the case of Egypt the Christian community was viewed not only as a religious minority but also as a political minority. In the perception of the Muslim Brotherhood the Christian political minority was a threat to the rule of their president, Morsi. They were made to understand that they should not reveal their critical political views.

I believe we are touching an essential difference between Christianity and Islam here. Whereas Christianity has a long tradition of separation between church and state, most strands of Islam do not recognize such a separation. For many Muslims, religion and politics should be intricately related. God's rule in the community, the *umma*, is established by political means, as it was in the Prophet Muhammad's Medina-period. Jesus, on the other hand, never aspired to be a political leader and hints at a separation in words such as "Give to Ceasar what is Ceasar's and to God what is God's" (Mark 12:17).

The Christian community has not always preserved a proper distance between state and religion, but in Muslim majority contexts Christians generally strive for a religiously neutral state. However, whenever Christians who live among Muslim majorities seek to separate between politics and religion, they risk being misunderstood or even being maltreated by Muslim fellow-citizens, who do not recognize the intentions and may misconstrue the political challenge as a religious threat.

Overcoming Gnosticism

Aside from the political make-up of Egypt, the attitude of the Evangelical churches also prevents it from being a fruitful minority. For many years the churches have focused on the spiritual life of their members. This was noticeable in sermons and in community activities. As pastors and preachers we did not speak about the role of Christians as citizens in the nation or the possible involvement of Christians in politics. We were a people of music and songs. Many of our hymns focused on heaven and the coming kingdom and they portrayed Christians as strangers in the world.

This attitude, which I call modern Gnosticism, contributed to a feeling of alienation from the world, which was found among many Christians. They hated the world and regarded this life as unimportant, basing themselves on the idea that we do not belong to it. We considered ourselves heavenly citizens and the earth as a mere bridge to eternity. I believe that this attitude has weakened the Christian community.

After the revolution of 2011, a new attitude towards citizenship began to appear. Prayers for the country and its future became an essential part of our worship. Many churches began to speak about politics and about the importance of participating in building our country. During the revolution against the regime of President Hosni Mubarak, we began to see the importance of participating in public events. In Cairo, a number of Evangelical churches served as hospitals during the revolutions. Those who were injured during the demonstrations received medical care in a church. When our church in Gad el-Seed was torched, we realized the danger of public involvement, but also the importance of our role in the country. We now believe that we are an effective minority and that we must participate in public events, in political elections and in social events. We must go outside the walls of our churches and show our presence in the different regions.

Conclusion

The Egyptians Christians are a very important minority. Egyptian Muslims may perceive them as a single political entity, a party in its own right, as was the case in the attacks of the Muslim Brotherhood on the churches. Christians must strive to change this perception. The only way to do this is by entering different political parties in which they cooperate with Muslims. If they do that, Christians will change the definition of minority. They will demonstrate that it does not mean to be a politically homogenous group with one agenda, but that it means to participate as an individual citizen in a specific political party with a specific political agenda.

In order to participate fruitfully in Egyptian society, Christians need to change their ideas about the world and about their country. They should live on earth not only as citizens of heaven, but be part of their society. They should respect their country and participate in shaping its future. At times, they may need to participate in demonstrations in order to do that. As Jesus said, we need to live as salt and light.

A Community of Hope in a Time of Violence

Christians in Lebanon and Syria

Wilbert and Rima van Saane-Nasrallah

This chapter addresses the impact of violence on the churches of Syria and Lebanon. It discusses the response of the churches and their leaders to the politically and sometimes religiously motivated violence in recent years. What does it mean to be a church in times of war and violence? What does it mean for pastoral care, worship, community building and relief work?

Rampant Violence

Violence is a reality that looms large in Iraq, Syria and Lebanon. Iraq has not known peace since the American invasion of 2003. Syria has been ravaged by war since 2011. The scale of the destruction in these two countries is immeasurable; the human suffering beyond words. Lebanon has not been exposed to such rampant violence in recent years. Nevertheless, the country faces a continuous spill-over of the Syrian war, as well as an unresolved conflict with Israel.

The violence has weakened the churches in Syria and Iraq. Before the wars in these countries began, the Christian demographic had already decreased due to voluntary emigration. In the past decade, it was forced migration that dealt an enormous blow to the Syrian and Iraqi church. Initially Christians were caught in the political turmoil, but more recently groups like the Islamic State (ISIS) deliberately targeted Christians and other religious minorities. As a result, thousands were internally displaced. Others had no other choice but to leave their country altogether.

Throughout history, Lebanon has been a safe haven for Christians. Today it is no different. The UNHCR calculated that the country hosted a staggering 1.3 million refugees by the beginning of 2015, the vast majority of which is from Syria and Iraq. This estimate was conservative; the real number of refugees was believed to be much higher. Among the displaced multitudes were thousands of Christians from Mosul, the Nineveh plains, Damascus, Homs, Deir ez-Zor, the region of Hassakeh, Aleppo, Kessab and other areas.

How do pastors, priests and other church leaders respond to the up-heaval in their countries? How does the violence impact the way they do pastoral care? What does it mean for the way they officiate worship ser-vices, administrate the sacraments, preach, and conduct Bible studies? With so many people on the move, how do they build community life? And, last but not least, how do they provide leadership to the church re-lief efforts?

Pastoral Presence in a Time of Terror

Leaders of the churches in the Middle East face a formidable enemy. Many people are terrified. You can hear it in conversations and in jokes. When people speak about plans for the future, they often jestingly add: "If IS does not get us before that . . ." or "If our country still exists . . ." Such remarks reveal a deep-seated insecurity. The sad fact is that there are reasonable grounds for Iraqi, Syrian and Lebanese Christians to dread the future.

Groups like IS wilfully instil fear in the population they seek to con-trol. Their media campaigns are designed to frighten people into submis-sion. Not only do they execute people, but they do it in gruesome ways and then circulate footage of their crimes in the media. Such videos may horrify and outrage viewers in other parts of the world, but what they do to people in the Middle East is erode a basic sense of security and trust. They feel unsafe in their own countries, in their own streets, and even inside their own homes.

How do pastoral workers address fear in the lives of their parishion-ers? First of all, it is their presence that counts. Church leaders in Syria and Iraq have been deeply aware of this. Many of them insist on staying with their communities at great personal risk. They know that their de-parture in this trying time will further undermine the confidence of their people. Their presence, on the other hand, will give their people courage and hope. In 2013, Father Frans van der Lugt, a Dutch Jesuit priest with a lifetime of service in Syria, remained with his small community in the besieged and starving city of Homs, even though he had the chance to leave. He paid with his life, but his dedication gave the morale of Chris-tians throughout Syria a tremendous boost.

On the eve of the massive attack on the Armenian town of Kessab in March 2014, its pastor was getting ready to pack his bags and head for a new assignment now that his term had finished. Yet, as his congregation evacuated their homes and towns, carrying nothing but the clothes they were wearing, the pastor changed his mind. He decided to stay with his flock. The only choice he saw was to be become displaced like his congregation. "I could have said 'my term is finished, I can go now,'" he said looking back. But that was the last thing on his mind. It was by staying with his congregation as a volunteer refugee that he brought courage into terrified hearts.

Perhaps trauma is even harder to address than fear. The fact is that the violence in Iraq, Syria and, to a lesser extent, Lebanon has traumatized thousands, if not millions. One deeply traumatized group are those middle-aged or older men who have seen their lives' work destroyed overnight by bombing, conquest, or economic downturn. They have left their homes, their memories and, in the process, their dignity. As refugees, they are no longer able to provide for their families. They are often too old for a new start on the labour market, which is hostile to foreigners in general. Many of them spend their days at home – is it home? – in silence. What comfort can pastoral workers offer these men?

Worship in a Time of Despair

Worshiping communities have changed on different levels due to war and terror. The most obvious change is the demographic one. Some parishes have seen most or all of their members leave, while others have experienced an influx of people who can no longer attend their home churches. Pastors and priests who used to minister to large numbers of church members now shepherd only a few, while their colleagues who previously led small churches are suddenly faced with capacity problems.

The destruction of churches and the population shifts have also resulted in an ecumenical shake-up. In a city like Aleppo, where many churches have been damaged or destroyed, Christians often worship in the nearest remaining church, even if that means crossing a denominational border. As a result, Protestant pastors find worshippers from Orthodox and Catholic backgrounds in their churches. Members of Protestant churches may too settle for an Orthodox or a Catholic church instead of travelling the dangerous road to a Protestant church.

While the size and composition of the worshiping congregation is not in the pastor's hands, the contents of the worship service are. Here the pastor faces intense existential choices. What Bible readings are appropriate to the current situation? What hymns will bring comfort and courage? How should the daily tragedies of country and city be addressed? In those terrible situations it is the words of Psalms that pastors use to voice the fear, anger, and trust that the congregation feels.

Special services, like weddings and funerals, often require pastoral inventiveness and courage. What does a pastor do when impassable roads prevent the groom's family from attending the engagement or the wedding? How does a pastor conduct a funeral in which he and the undertaker are the only attendants? What to do if during a funeral a fresh round of shelling starts? And what if the church's cemetery is inaccessible due to the fighting?

When church leaders are in a predicament on how to comfort their congregations, consoling words from the Bible may present themselves. As Jesus promised, "when the Spirit of truth comes, he will guide you into all the truth" (John 16:13 NRSV). Pastors from the warzones in Syria and Iraq testify that words from Scripture have sustained them and their congregations in powerful and wondrous ways in trying times.

Community Building in a Time of Displacement

On an even more basic level, church leaders in Iraq and Syria are struggling to keep their communities together. Their people are on the move and the direction of this movement is generally away from the Middle East. Among the displaced from Baghdad, Mosul, Nineveh, Deir ez-Zor, Hassakeh, Aleppo and Homs, many have emigrated or are preparing to do so. Their destinations are countries such as Canada, the United States, Sweden, Germany, Armenia, and Australia. If they have relatives in such countries, they try to join them. If that is not the case, they register as refugees and wait for the UNHCR to offer them an opportunity. Among the Armenians, many choose to move to Armenia, even if they know that building a new life there will not be easy.

Some Iraqi and Syrian church leaders have criticised Western countries for their readiness to receive Christian migrants. The Chaldean Patriarch, Louis Raphael Sako, has repeatedly said that he believes Christians should stay, in spite of all the danger. According to Sako, Christians have "an identity, a role, a history" in the Middle East, which they must not abandon. He estimates that the Iraqi Christian population has been reduced from 1.2 million before the American invasion in 2003 to less than four hundred thousand today. Such estimates are not yet available for Syria, but they are undoubtedly equally dramatic. In August 2014, it was estimated that out of the two hundred-fifty thousand Christians of the city Aleppo only one hundred thousand remained. In 2015, the violence in Aleppo only grew and many more have left the city. Church leaders are witnessing the gradual disintegration of their communities. In the autumn of 2014, the leaders of the Protestant churches in Syria and Lebanon issued an appeal to partner churches in which they declared a "state of emergency, in order to preserve what remains of the Christian – and moderate non-Christian – presence in the Middle East, and to circumvent its complete demise."

So important is the Christian presence to church leaders in Iraq and Syria that in the year 2015 some provided regular financial aid to those who remain in the warzones. Christians who returned to ravaged cities like Homs or Kessab received practical support – water, meals, and supplies needed for their homes – from the churches. The churches often relied on partner churches and organizations in other countries for resources. They are aware that they cannot maintain the Christian presence in the Middle East by such means, but they hope for a better future and attempt to bridge the time until that future has arrived.

The displacement of the Christians of Iraq and Syria tests the creativity of their leaders. While some see only the deprivation of their communities, others feel called to engage in new ministries. When Homs was a battleground, many of its Christians settled in Wadi Nasara, a hilly region near Syria's Mediterranean coast. Protestant church leaders soon realized that this community of uprooted people needed to be served. Schooling for their children was a priority, so they provided temporary educational facilities in Wadi Nasara. In Lebanon, Evangelical groups, perceiving the mental and spiritual upheaval of Syrian refugees, have evangelized and fostered new forms of church life among them. Time will tell if the despair of the refugee camps will result in a remarkable turn to Christ.

Church leaders throughout the region realize that in order to protect, maintain and build their communities, they need strong bonds with moderate Muslims. That is why many of them continue to invest in good neighbourly relations with Islamic leaders. They do this on a practical, but also on a more theoretical level. In the besieged city of Aleppo, a pastor and a sheikh cooperate to provide water to their neighbourhood. In Beirut, the Near East School of Theology maintains a theological dialogue with Muslim centres of learning, to foster rapprochement and mutual respect.

Since Christian communities have very little political power, it is part of their mission to accompany moderate Muslims in their struggle to preserve democracy, human rights and religious freedom, which are increasingly threatened by jihadist groups. Thankfully, many moderate Muslims have stated that they do not wish the Christians of the Middle East to disappear. In December 2014, even scholars from Al-Azhar in Cairo urged

Christians "to stay rooted in their homelands and to weather this wave of terrorism".

Relief Work in a Time of Destruction

The sheer size and the complexity of the catastrophe in Iraq and Syria are unparalleled. UN officials have called it "the worst humanitarian crisis in the twenty-first century". It is not clear how many Syrians and Iraqis have fled their countries or are internally displaced, but it concerns millions. Since the conquest of large swathes of Iraq and Syria by the jihadist groups like IS, al-Nusra, and al-Qaeda, the need has dramatically increased.

The churches of the Middle East have been involved in relief work since the very beginning of the crisis. There is no Christian denomination that has remained unaffected by the violence. Since charity starts at home, many Christians have cared for victims from their own denominations. Presbyterians have organized relief for Presbyterians; Chaldeans for Chaldeans; Armenians for Armenians. Most church-affiliated relief work is, however, not exclusive. Generous aid has been provided across denominational and religious lines. In the area of Hassakeh, for example, the Presbyterian Church was instrumental in assisting the Chaldean refugees, while in Beirut the Protestant Church was quick to offer help to the Assyrians.

The nature of the relief work varies according to the need. In case of displacement, there is a need for almost everything: temporary housing, food, clothes, fuel for heating and cooking, schooling for children. In warzones, there is a need for electricity, fresh water and often food supplies as well. Many creative solutions have been found to meet the need. In Aleppo, old artesian wells in church yards were reopened after IS took over the water company and cut off the Christian parts of the city. In Wadi Nasara, instead of relying on food parcels, the church provided food vouchers in cooperation with local store owners, so that people were able to select their own supplies and the local economy was stimulated.

Large international relief organizations have provided much assistance, but they often either arrived late on the scene or were simply not able to access the conflict areas. The presence of the churches in villages and neighbourhoods, as well as their networks, have given them a very detailed idea of the actual needs. Church leaders are often in a uniquely suitable position to offer relief, as they are trusted by many. Consequently, church leaders have found themselves in charge of large-scale relief operations. They are not trained for such work, but they cannot ignore the need. Often the best results are achieved when a local church works in partnership with an international organization.

Providing relief is messy work and comes with dilemmas. Do we provide aid to people who support factions that are in fact our enemies? Do we facilitate people's departure from the war-torn countries or do we strive to keep them in the country?

Hungry, Naked Stranger

In spite of all the horrors the war has brought, it is heart-warming to see that Christians in the affected areas are coming together. They visit each other's churches, they stand together, and they speak with a united voice. An Armenian Orthodox bishop from Syria recently commented: "I wish that we had achieved this degree of unity a long time ago. It is a shame that it took a war to make us grow in unity."

When everything is taken away, people realize that they can only depend on God. They look for meaning in their misfortunes and find it in faith. Although loss and pain prompted some to turn away from God, many others confessed that the crisis made them rely on God and strengthened their faith.

A nine year-old boy surprised his Sunday School teacher in Beirut by explaining his reasons for preparing a gift parcel for the refugee children: "I can see Jesus in them," he said. War and destruction can reveal a lot of evil, but they can also make us aware of Christ's presence among us and compel us to respond. War has destroyed many churches. It has shaken the faith of many. It has damaged and scarred lives forever. But, in the midst of all this, communities of faith are rising to the challenge, encouraging each other and testifying to a God who is greater than death.

Perseverance in a Time of Persecution

Christians in Central Asia

Anneta Vyssotskaia

This case study is about the little known story of the silent suffering of Christians in Central Asia. They are facing hardships on many levels, and the situation is not improving. This chapter lists the types of persecution that Christians suffer from and tells three heart-breaking stories. However, it also highlights that Christians draw strength from their faith in Christ.

A Secret Believer

B. was the fifth child in a Muslim family in Central Asia. He was born with severe physical disabilities. When B. turned seven years old, his father abandoned his family and B. was raised by his mother in poverty. He experienced a lot of rejection because of his disability. As a young teenager he was sent to a children's hospital for medical treatment. At the hospital, he met some Christian believers who shared about Jesus and showed genuine love and care for the patients. He became a secret believer, never sharing about his new faith. In times of difficulties he called to Jesus for help. As he grew older he found some Christians living in the neighbourhood. He started to attend church meetings, read the Bible, and grew in his faith; he was also baptized with water. When his family heard that he had become a Christian, his sisters and their husbands became very angry. They beat him and tore his Bible into pieces. It did not stop B. from going to the church where he found a truly loving family. His Christian faith helps him to stay strong despite his disability and rejection. This is just one of a multitude of similar stories of Christians facing persecution in Central Asia.

The History of Christianity in Central Asia

Central Asia is a vast region including five countries which were once part of the Soviet Union and became independent countries after the fall of the communist regime: Uzbekistan, Kazakhstan, Kyrgyzstan, Tajikistan, and Turkmenistan. Its total population exceeds sixty-five million and may be divided into over one hundred ethnic groups.

According to legend, Christianity came to Central Asia in the first century. Ancient documents confirm that it was well established there by the fourth century. It was wiped out by Islam and Buddhism around the fourteenth century and all but disappeared. The majority of Central Asians know nothing about their Christian roots and consider Islam to be the only religion of their ancestors.

Christianity came back to Central Asia in the form of the Russian Orthodox religion of the Russian officials and farmer migrants and the religion of Evangelical Christians who moved to the region as a result of the persecution by the Russian Empire in the nineteenth century. During times of militant atheism in the Soviet period, Christians were persecuted along with adherents of other religions. In the early 1990s, after the fall of communism, these countries experienced Christian revival and many people turned to God.

Islam on the Rise

Very soon after these revivals began, restrictions of religious freedom and different forms of persecution were reintroduced. Today the governments of the Central Asian countries give preference to particular forms of Islam and some other religions, while followers of unapproved faiths face many constraints and often persecution. The growing influence of Islam can be easily seen from the increasing number of mosques and people attending them. In Kyrgyzstan, for instance, the number of mosques more than doubled in twenty years, from about one thousand in the mid-1990s to 2,200 in 2012.

At present the Russian Orthodox Church, the Roman Catholic Church and various Protestant denominations constitute Christianity in Central Asia. Christianity is a small minority in this predominantly Muslim region. Four Central Asian countries were included in the Open Doors World Watch List of the fifty countries where Christians experienced different forms of persecution in 2015. Kyrgyzstan was not included in that list in 2015, which does not mean that persecution does not take place in that country.

Persecution by the State at Different Levels

As religious minorities in Central Asia, Christians may face persecution at different levels, especially those of family, community, and state. While persecution of Russian Orthodox and Roman Catholic Christians rarely occurs, Evangelical Christians often face opposition. One of the reasons is that they actively share their faith with their Muslim neighbours.

The greatest pressure is on Christians from a Muslim background. They are seen as traitors and as a shame for their families and for the Muslim community at large. All ethnic Turkmen, Tajiks, Uzbeks, Kazakhs and Kyrgyz are supposed to be Muslims, and experience a lot of pressure and persecution if they become followers of Jesus Christ.

The situation differs from country to country. Uzbekistan is the fifteenth hardest place for Christians to live according to the Open Doors World Watch List, Turkmenistan comes twentieth, Kazakhstan forty-second, and Tajikistan forty-fifth. However, the trend is that restriction of religious freedom is constantly increasing in Central Asia. Common forms of persecution and restriction of religious freedom are:

- Laws that forbid Christian meetings outside the buildings of registered churches;
- Restrictions on printing, storing and distributing religious literature;
- Prohibition of Biblical education of children and adults;
- Difficulty or impossibility of getting registration for churches;
- Police raids of Christian churches and believers' homes;
- Confiscation of Christian literature and equipment like computers;
- Fines for the illegal gathering and storing of Christian literature;
- Detention and imprisonment;
- Dismissal of Christians from employment in government institutions, especially common for school teachers;
- Expulsion of students from state universities if they convert.

Persecution by Muslim Communities

Muslim background Christians and non-ethnic believers in Christ who share their faith with Muslims are a special target of persecution from the Muslim community. Children experience persecution alongside their Christian parents. The persecution can also affect the non-Christian family members of Christian believers. In some cases, Christians have said that their non-Christian family members experienced persecution in an attempt to use them to put pressure on them when it could not be done directly. Among the most common forms of persecution from the community are:

- Local campaigns by Muslim religious leaders against Christians in an attempt to ignite religious hatred against them among the local Muslim population;

- Threats, beatings, stoning and in rare cases murder;
- Discrimination in the workplace, such as exclusion from the use of communal services like the water supply;
- Rejection, harassment and marginalization;
- In some countries Christians or their family members are denied proper burial at the local cemeteries.

Persecution by the Family

For Central Asian people the family is of extreme importance. Often Christian believers face a choice between their faith in Jesus and their family. Being rejected by the family is the most painful experience for many Christians from Muslim backgrounds. Some common forms of persecution are:

- Threats, shaming, and persuasion in an attempt to make a person convert back to Islam;
- Abduction and home imprisonment of Christians by their family members;
- Beatings and other physical abuse;
- Rape of Christian women;
- Total rejection by family members.

Three Real Life Situations

Often it is easier to be a Christian in big cities than it is in the villages. Here are three examples of real life situations from Central Asia that illustrate this point.

A Muslim family in a remote village converted to Christianity. They experienced threats and rejection by the local community. Their children were not allowed to travel to the school in another village by school bus for a long period of time, because the people in their village did not want their children to have contact with Christians. The children were not able to attend school during that period. Finally, the government intervened because education is compulsory. Even though the children were able to continue their studies, the tension remained and both children and parents continued to receive threats.

A Christian camp for youth from a non-registered church held in a remote location was raided by police. All participants were detained and held for several hours in a police station. They were forced to write explanatory notes. All Christian books and equipment were confiscated. One young Christian from the ethnic majority was separated from the rest of the group and special pressure was put on him to reject his Christian faith. He was threatened and physically tortured, and was not given food or water for several days in extremely hot weather. He was locked in a prison cell for fifteen days. While he was almost unconscious, hovering between life and death, he saw a vision of Jesus coming to his cell, comforting and strengthening him. He experienced tremendous peace from God. After fifteen days he was released from prison. While he was in prison his church prayed for him unceasingly. The church also helped him through the healing and rehabilitation process. His faith became stronger and he currently serves as a pastor.

A university student from a Muslim family became a Christian. When his family in a village heard the news they abducted him and shut him in a room for many months. They told him they would not let him out until he converted back to Islam. They took away all his possessions, including his Bible, and almost all his clothes. They gave him food and water but deprived him of all his freedom. He was threatened and beaten. His mother, whom he loves very much, tearfully pleaded with him to return to Islam. Finally, he managed to escape and he returned to the city. His relationship with his family is broken.

What Helps Christians to Stand Strong in Faith?

In spite of all the hardships, the church in Central Asia has not disappeared. Almost deprived of support from the government, the Muslim community and international organizations, they rely mostly on their spiritual resources. These resources help them to persevere in their faith.

- **The reality of God's presence and his help:** Many Central Asian believers experience God's presence in special ways, through miracles, visions, signs and wonders, healings, pregnancies of previously infertile women, and in other ways.
- **New freedom in Christ:** People experience liberation from addiction to drugs, unforgiving attitudes, self-rejection, feelings of shame, and fear. Many Christians say they experience peace and joy that they did not know before they met Christ.
- **Strong relationships and regular fellowship with other church members:** Christian churches are a new family and a new community for the new believer. There is a strong sense of belonging to each other and to God through Jesus Christ.

- **Growing in the knowledge of the Word of God:** The full Bible translation is not always available in the local languages, but this is a work in progress. Central Asian people are predominantly oral learners, even though they can read. They like hearing Bible stories and memorizing them. The stories of the shining faith of the early church Christians during the dark periods of persecution provide an encouragement and an example for the modern day Christians in Central Asia.
- **Strong prayer life:** This is a real strength of the church in Central Asia. They often combine prayer with fasting for long periods of time, from one day to one week and up to forty days in some cases.
- **Focusing on God and his will** in the situation of persecution and economic hardship.
- **The historical example of the perseverance of the Christian Church in the USSR** during the seventy-year period of severe persecution serves as an encouragement to many believers who experience persecution in our days.

Despite the persecution the church is growing in Central Asia as the church leaders are focused on mission both inside and outside the region.

Questions for Further Reflection

From which three groups do Central Asian Christians experience persecution? In which way does it affect the life of all Christians in that region?

From which group does the persecution come in each of the three real-life situations described in this chapter? How does it affect the life of the Christians? What can help Christians to stand strong in their faith in each particular situation?

When a person with a Muslim background becomes a Christian, how can other Christians in the church help him or her to be prepared for persecution?

If your Christian friend from a Muslim background calls you and says that his family is threatening to force him to leave his home unless he rejects his Christian faith, how would you respond to this?

Can you suggest some of the reasons why it can be easier to be a Christian in a big city than in the countryside?

Between Harmony and Conflict

The Evangelical Community of Albania

Andi Dina

This chapter addresses the issue of religious freedom in Albania, both on the level of denominations and on the level of the individual. It traces the long and difficult road to official state recognition of the Evangelical churches and uses several life stories to illustrate the limitations on religious freedom that Albanian Christians face, especially when it comes to conversion.

Ardian's Story

Ardian grew up in a pious Muslim family in the city of Tirana. In spite of his religious upbringing, by the time he was eighteen Ardian fell prey to drug abuse, gambling and depression. In that state, he came to know Christ in a miraculous way and he completely surrendered his life to God. Ardian started to share his newfound faith with his family and friends. After a few weeks, his brother and his parents came to faith in Christ. Like Ardian, they testified that they had become Christians and that Christ had set them free. Their enthusiasm and commitment irritated their extended family and they faced rejection from cousins, neighbours and friends. Nevertheless, they continued to attend church regularly and tried to ignore all the curses, insults and rejections. They also continued to show love to the people around them and over the past three years their situation has radically improved. They now have a very good relationship with their relatives, neighbours and friends. In spite of all the hardships they encountered, they demonstrated that Christ has changed their lives for good. Ardian and his family are faithful followers of Christ and their good testimony has affected their Muslim environment. It is their dream that everyone around them comes to know Christ, but until that day they have chosen to love their Muslim relatives, friends and neighbours.

Ardian's story is characteristic for the situation of the Evangelical community in Albania. They navigate between acceptance and suppression, between harmony and conflict. This chapter will describe the position of Evangelical Christians in some detail. It will trace the road to official recognition of Evangelicals as a denomination, but also underline that in spite of this, Evangelicals continue to experience pressure, especially when they engage in evangelism. Before describing this ambiguous situation of Evangelicals, a general sketch of the religious demography of Albania will be provided.

The Religious Landscape of Albania

According to the 2011 census, almost 60 percent of Albania's population adheres to Islam. Islam came to Albania when the country was part of the Ottoman Empire and many converted to Islam. The majority of Albanian Muslims are Sunni (almost 57 percent). A small minority of just over 2 percent belongs to the Bektashi Shia community. Christianity is practiced by nearly 17 percent of the population, making it the second largest religion in the country. The remainder of the population is either irreligious or belongs to other religious groups. Decades of state atheism which ended in 1991 brought a decline in religious practice in all traditions.

It is interesting to note that the statistics are not uncontested. A recent demographic study of the Pew Research Center put the percentage of Muslims in Albania at almost 80 percent. A recent Gallup poll, on the other hand, suggest that only 43% of the Albanians is Muslim, whereas the Christians make up 34 percent(of which 19 percent is Eastern Orthodox and 15 percent Catholic). This poll estimates that 23 percent of the population is atheist or nonreligious. The figures of the 2011 census take a middle ground between the Pew and the Gallup estimates. The census differentiates Catholics (10.03 percent), Orthodox (6.75 percent), Evangelicals (0.14 percent), and other Christians (0.07 percent).

Islam in Albania may be divided in three main streams: nominal Islam, traditional Islam and radical Islam. Under nominal Muslims I count people who do not go to the mosque, do not read the Koran and do not make rituals and commandments part of their daily life. Most Albanian Muslims fall into this category.

In my typology, traditional Muslims are people who do not only claim to be Muslim, but also take a lively interest in their religion. They strive to know more about their faith, about the Koran and about the rules and rituals that pertain to Islam. They are not necessarily very committed Muslims, but they are certainly candidates to become part of the radical category.

Radical Islam is a newcomer to the Albanian religious scene. Cells of radical Muslims have been identified since 1993, but radical Islam has grown particularly fast over the past decade. Radical Muslims are obviously very committed to their faith. They do everything in their power to see that Islamic rules are applied and that the appropriate rituals are conducted. They read the Koran, they faithfully attend mosque and they try to persuade others to meet their standards.

Interestingly, radical Albanian Muslims do not use the verb "to convert" for their proselytizing activities. Instead, they prefer the term "to revert" because they believe that every human being is born a Muslim, but that people are deceived and led astray during their lifetime. In their opinion, it is the duty of every true Muslim to bring others back to the only true religion, to make them return. Today we find groups of radical Muslims in every Albanian city. They are easily identifiable by their robes and the long beards that the men sport. Their numbers are growing.

The Long Road towards State Recognition

Since 2012, the Albanian Evangelical Church has been an officially recognized denomination: the fifth such community in Albania after Roman Catholics, Orthodox, Muslims and Jews. The process leading up to the registration by the Albanian state was long and difficult. The Evangelical Church's minority status was one of the main barriers: Evangelicals had little political influence. Often it was difficult to arrange meetings with politicians and government officials. Although there was a governmental committee for religious denominations, it was hard to find a voice that advocated for the Evangelical community.

In light of the long history of the Evangelical community it was surprising that state recognition presented such a challenge. The community traces its origins in Albania back to the late nineteenth century, when the country was still part of the Ottoman Empire. In the 1890s, a Protestant congregation and a school for girls were established in the city of Korce, and later, in 1920, a school for boys was added. Aside from their role in education, Evangelicals played a very important part in the alphabet commission and in the independence of Albania in 1912. The growth of the Albanian Protestant community was, however, minimal during the 1920s, 1930s and 1940s.

The Evangelical contribution to Albanian culture and politics was pushed into oblivion by the communist regime. In 1944, Enver Hoxha came to power and immediately began implementing rigid Stalinist reforms. The communist government's campaign to eradicate all religion culminated in the year 1967, when many religious leaders were executed or imprisoned and Orthodox, Catholic, Muslim and Protestant sanctuaries were shut down or converted for uses other than worship. In the two decades that followed Albania was an isolated nation in which religion was prohibited. The ban on religion was finally lifted in 1991.

After the fall of communism Protestantism grew, but it proved very difficult to promote in Albania. At times there was outright discrimination of Evangelical Christians. The majority of the population viewed Evangelical Christianity as an imported religion from the West, especially from America. Some even used offensive vocabulary, accusing Evangelicals of being spies of the Americans. Evangelicals were often referred to as a group similar to the Jehovah Witnesses or the Mormons, as apostates, or as people who had sold their soul to non-Albanians.

It took a campaign of twenty years to have the Evangelical community recognized. The Evangelical Alliance of Albania (EAA) had a vital role in this process. The EAA was founded in 1993 in the capital Tirana, and represents most of the Christian churches and Evangelical organizations in Albania. It was the EAA that sustained prayer, lobbying and advocacy for recognition. It was the EEA that signed the recognition agreement with the Albanian government in November 2011, a historic moment for the Albanian Evangelical Christian community. Apart from the key contribution of the EAA, there was pressure from the US Embassy, Christian parliamentarians of the European Union, and the World Evangelical Alliance. Through the media, Akil Pano, Evangelical pastor and general secretary of the EAA, created awareness in civil society about the Evangelical struggle for recognition.

The Quest for Harmony between the Religions

Representatives of other religious groups had very little input in the process of recognition of the Evangelical community. The Bektashi community had an open and positive attitude towards the Evangelicals throughout. Unfortunately, the same could not be said of the other religious communities, like the Sunnis, the Catholics and the Orthodox.

After the official recognition the Evangelical community (represented by the EAA) has been part of many interreligious meetings, interfaith dialogues, government-sponsored activities, religious and nonreligious celebrations. These events have helped religious leaders and communities to know each other and to build relationship that foster tolerance and harmony.

The quest for harmony is a recent trend in the country. Over the past decade, virtually all religious, political, and social actors, as well as governmental and non-governmental institutions have proclaimed concord and tolerance between the religions as a value crucial to Albania. A large number of interfaith events have been devoted to this subject.

Religious tolerance is pertinent in Albania because of the rise of radical Islam. Converts to Christianity from Islam have given first-hand testimonies of attending mosques where hate sermons were delivered and where Jews and Christians were denounced. Such discourse is found especially in areas where radical Muslims are the predominant group. One person I interviewed told me: "I could not understand why every Friday during the main meeting I would hear them speaking against Christians and Jews."

Evangelicals welcome the public emphasis on harmony and tolerance, because they have experienced and are still experiencing intolerance. On the grassroots level they find that religious freedom is still very problematic, especially when they engage in evangelism – an important trait of Evangelical Christianity – and when their evangelism leads to the conversion of Muslims to Christianity.

Opposition to Evangelical Christianity

Over the past years, there has been opposition to Evangelical Christianity in varying degrees. The most explicit case of religious hatred towards a Christian leader occurred in the city of Delvina in March 2010, when a radical imam attacked the pastor of an Evangelical Church with a knife. This pastor was very active in evangelism and instrumental in the conversion of a number of Muslims to Christianity. The imam was trying to put a stop to that, but the pastor survived.

Another example of opposition is that of a church planting programme in the city of Tirana that started in October 2013. A team of Christian volunteers committed to be part of a church planting team and started in a residential area with ten thousand inhabitants of whom about 90 percent is Muslim. The area has five mosques, but there is no Christian church. In this community all categories mentioned above are present: nominal Muslims, traditional Muslims and radical Muslims. The church team visited people and organized meetings for children with games and a Bible story. When an assistant-imam from the area was informed about the meetings, he came and threatened the team. He broke up the meeting, destroyed the games and was violent with some children. He continued to warn the community and incite people against the small Christian team. He did everything in his power to prevent the team from returning. The home church of the team prayed intensively and the next week the team visited the area again. The volunteers were surprised to see that this time nobody stopped or harmed them. For eighteen months, they continued to visit families, to preach the gospel and to talk about the love of God. The result of their efforts is that a church came into existence in this area.

Individuals who convert from Islam to Christianity often face serious challenges. Fifteen years ago Genti (not her real name) and her family turned to Christianity and joined an Evangelical Church. This is the story of what happened after her conversion.

> I come from a traditional Muslim family. We strongly associated with our religious tradition, although we did not observe all the rituals. My village is located in the Northeast of Albania and has many mosques, imams and Muslim leaders. When my family and I started following Christ the reaction was instant. Many times the leader of the village, a traditional Muslim, personally came to communicate messages that were more like threats: "If you do not revert to Islam, it is better for you to leave the village. If you do not leave, we will burn your house and will not allow your family to be buried in this village." This threat was not void; when my grandmother died the religious leaders prevented us from burying her in the village cemetery. The conflict became so sharp that my uncle threatened to kill one of the religious leaders. After this serious incident we were able to bury our grandmother. At times Christian missionaries visited us, only to find the road blocked with stones and thorns when they were trying to leave the village. The message was clear: missionaries were not welcome in the village. My father worked far away from home and he came to visit us for about six weeks every year. Every time he came home he had to leave earlier because the pressure of the religious leaders. Most of the people hated us at that time. Today, many years later, some people in the village think and behave in the same way, but many others have changed their opinion about us.

The stories of Genti, Ardian and many others demonstrate that conversion is a very problematic issue in Albanian interreligious relations. Because of the value they attach to evangelism and religious transformation, Evangelicals find themselves at odds with Muslim communities that view religious conversion as apostasy and are prepared to use violence to prevent their members from converting.

A Christian Minority among a Muslim Majority

As Albanian Evangelical Christians, we live in harmony with nominal Muslims. In general, religion is not an obstacle in building relationships with nominal Muslims. They do not even object to marriages between Muslims and Christians. As Evangelicals, we talk about the gospel of Jesus Christ freely with people who belong to this group. This is somewhat more difficult among people who are part of what I called traditional Islam. Faith discussion may lead to serious tension here. That is why we approach members of this group with care and we avoid giving them the impression that we are trying to convert them.

As Evangelical Christians, we find it very difficult to build relationships with radical Muslims, and we are not able to win their trust. In our experience, they view us as people deceived by Satan until the moment when we will "revert" to Islam.

The Evangelical churches and communities of Albania try to live by the teachings of Christ to love our neighbour as ourselves. We believe we are called to love and not to hate, to bless and not to curse, and even to love our enemy. Generally speaking, the response of the Christian communities to opposition has been love, forgiveness and tolerance. We have to admit, however, that at times Christians have been intimidated when facing the threats of radical Muslims. In spite of the official recognition, the Evangelical community is still caught between harmony and conflict.

Coping with Social Exclusion

Evangelicals in Kosovo

Rik Lubbers

This contribution provides insight into how the Protestant Evangelical Church takes its place as a religious minority in the Islamic context of Kosovo. Although religious freedom is safeguarded by Kosovo's constitution, Protestant Evangelicals face discrimination on various levels. This chapter describes these struggles and the way Protestant Evangelicals cope with them.

Religion in Kosovo

Kosovo is a small country in the Western Balkans. Since 1999, after the most recent Balkan war, it has been de facto a separate state from Serbia. On 17 February 2008, the government of Kosovo officially declared the Republic of Kosovo an independent state. Islam is the dominant religion in this youngest country of Europe with around 1.9 million inhabitants. Over 90 percent of the Albanians in Kosovo call themselves Muslim.[5] Even when Kosovar Albanians adhere to a nominal form of Islam, they consider it an integral part of their identity. An expression which can be heard regularly in Kosovo is: "I am Kosovar Albanian and therefore a Muslim."

The question of how religion impacts daily life is less important for many in Kosovo. Most Kosovar Albanians call themselves Muslim, but they do not practise an Islamic life style and they appear as secular.[6] There is, however, a small Islamic opposition movement, which emphasizes a more conscious form of Islam and the associated religious practice.

Alongside the Muslim majority, there are two other dominant religious groups: The Serbian Orthodox Church and the Roman Catholic

---

[5]   Many sources estimate that 90-95 percent of the Kosovar people is Muslim, but there is a lack of official and reliable resources. See e.g. G. Duijzings, *Religion and the Politics of Identity in Kosovo* (London: Hurst & Company, 2000), 15.

[6]   T. Judah, *Kosovo: What Everyone Needs to Know* (Oxford: Oxford University Press, 2008), 8, calls Albanians "very secular people" but adds that "the overwhelming majority of Kosovo Albanians are of Muslim background."

Church. Orthodox believers were already few in number before the latest conflict between the Serbs and Albanians in 1998-1999. After the massive emigration of Serbs after the war, their number has further decreased. Nevertheless, Kosovo remains a religiously important area with active monasteries that attract many faithful Serbs and tourists each year.

Kosovo also has a Roman Catholic minority. It is estimated that there are around sixty thousand Catholics. Many villages are completely Catholic, in contrast to the surrounding area which is Islamic. Catholics are more or less accepted because of the historical roots of the Catholic Church in Kosovo. Ethnically they are Albanians, just like their Muslim compatriots.

In addition to these three dominant religions,[7] Kosovo has around forty independent Protestant Evangelical Churches, which are mostly united under one umbrella organization, the Kosovo Protestant Evangelical Church (KPEC). The KPEC has been a member of the World Evangelical Alliance since 2009. These forty churches are, on average, small with around thirty-five to forty-five members. In Pristina, the capital city of Kosovo, there are some bigger churches with around 80 members. These city churches often have many students among their members. The KPEC has indicated that there are ten to fifteen thousand Protestant Evangelicals in Kosovo, a very high estimate. Even half this number may be too generous. At any rate, the Evangelicals are a small minority in the predominantly Islamic context of Kosovo.

Following Kosovo's declaration of independence in 2008, the government accepted a constitution that includes freedom of religion. Later, upon the insistence of the KPEC, the Protestant Evangelical Church was mentioned by name in the constitution: *"To all religions and their communities in Kosovo including the Islamic Community of Kosovo, the Serbian Orthodox Church, the Catholic Church, the Hebrew Belief Community, and the Evangelical Church, shall be offered any kind of protection and opportunity in order to have rights and freedom provided for by this law. Religious communities in Kosovo enjoy all the rights with this Law."*[8]

Thus, Kosovar legislation protects the members of all religions. People have the right to gather together and the right to confess their faith.

---

[7] Other religious movements include Jews, Jehovah's Witnesses and Mormons, but their numbers are so small that they are often not mentioned in literature and data information about religious life in Kosovo.

[8] Article 5.4 of the Law on Freedom of Religion no. 48 (2006), cited from the website of KPEC. See: http://www.kishaprotestante.net/index.php, consulted in March 2015.

However, there is a big difference between the formal protection by law and everyday practice.

Social Persecution

In spite of the formal protection, Evangelicals face social exclusion. This expresses itself in tension within families, a disadvantaged position on the labour market – for example in job applications – difficulties in registering properties such as church buildings and the lack of Protestant cemeteries, which makes it impossible for Evangelicals to conduct Christian funerals. Up to the present day, Kosovar Evangelicals have not suffered from physical persecution, but the discrimination that confronts them may be labelled as social persecution.

What are the reasons for the social persecution of Kosovar Evangelicals? First, and most importantly, there is a widespread feeling among the population of Kosovo that Evangelicals are betrayers of their own people and nation. This feeling is projected on to all Christians, regardless of their denomination. Orthodox, Catholics and Evangelicals are, in the general perception, all one Christian movement. These feelings of betrayal have roots in the long history of the Balkans, but recently the latest Balkan war, the so-called Kosovo War in 1998-1999, fuelled these feelings again. During this war, many Albanians were killed in the name of the Serbian government, which has a close connection to the Serbian Orthodox Church.

Second, while Roman Catholics are generally accepted, because they have lived alongside Muslims for centuries, a lot of Kosovar Albanians see the Protestant Evangelical movement as a sect that may have a negative influence on the Kosovar society. The Evangelical denomination is often unknown and therefore unloved.

A third reason why Evangelical Albanians face social persecution is their message. Evangelicals are spreading the gospel as good news to everyone, including the country's ethnic minorities. Officially all ethnic minorities enjoy protection under the law, but in practical, daily life, some minorities are subordinated. Many Albanians in Kosovo find it hard to accept that Evangelicals care for minority groups such as the Roma people, and treat them as equals to Albanians and other ethnicities.

Finally social persecution is related to the fact that the Albanian culture in Kosovo is strongly determined by honour and shame. When a member of a Muslim family becomes an Evangelical Christian, the family finds itself in a very difficult position. The conversion of one family member results in immediate complications for the whole family within their village or city, as the honour of the family is at stake.

So, despite the formal freedom of religion and the protection by the Kosovar constitution, we observe social persecution of Protestant Evangelicals in Kosovo. It is not surprising, therefore, that Kosovo also has secret believers in Christ.

Coping with Social Persecution

The believers in Kosovo cope with and counter social persecution both on the national and the local levels. The KPEC, as the umbrella organization for Protestant Evangelicals in Kosovo, represents the churches in the public sphere. The local church and local believers also play their part. We will look at both aspects.

The KPEC has its lobby in Pristina, and it regularly lobbies the government, keeping religious freedom on the political agenda and within the public sphere. It advocates for the churches in matters such as the registration of buildings, the taxes on buildings and workers, the protection of Christians and Christian buildings especially during Christian holidays and festivals, and the registration of local Christian workers and international workers as missionaries. The national office of the KPEC also participates in organizing interfaith dialogues. A good example of the KPEC's advocacy is that it recently started to draw attention to the need for Christian burial sites. In such ways the KPEC office in Pristina ensures the presence of the Protestant Evangelical churches in the public sphere. It calls for implementation of the official protection offered by the law, and engages with politicians, governmental institutions and law enforcement powers.

Alongside the KPEC's ministry in the public sphere, the local church communities deal more directly with the everyday difficulties and struggles of Christians. When a convert is perceived as a traitor by his or her family, local churches provide pastoral assistance and advice. There are many other issues related to the perception of Christians that local Christians and local churches grapple within their city or village context, none of which are easy.

Christian churches exist for the glory of God. One of the ways in which they glorify God is by being edified, built up as disciples of Jesus.[9] In the context of Kosovo, church edification is very challenging. Congre-

---

[9]   See: M.J. Erickson, *Christian Theology*, vol. 3 (Grand Rapids, MI: Baker Book House, 1985), 1051-1068.

gations normally meet once a week, but many members of the church attend meetings irregularly. In most churches a small group of believers regularly comes together, while a large group does not have the possibility to do so. Either their work prevents them from attending the meetings, or they fear the negative response from their families and neighbours. Their absence from the gatherings means they are not in the place where spiritual edification, or encouragement happens.

As a missionary in this context I think an alternative worth exploring is to either visit church members in their homes or, if that is not possible, to meet them at other places and times. Protestant Evangelical churches need to look for creative ways of edification and discipleship. They need to think of alternative ways of being church if they wish to equip and encourage these often young and inexperienced believers.

Another opportunity for edification and discipleship is conferences and training weeks. These events are often organized in cooperation with the national office of the KPEC or foreign organizations and churches. Conferences are remarkably well attended by local believers, but often not contextually sensitive. The support, not only financial, of partner churches and agencies will be crucial for the KPEC to establish a more permanent and contextually sensitive training facility for believers in Kosovo.

Apart from the struggles related to the minority status of Evangelical Christians, they also share the daily struggles of all Kosovars: poverty, a high unemployment rate, crime, the scourge of the mafia, human trafficking, corruption, illiteracy and the ongoing practice of blood feuds. The discontent among Kosovar citizens is increasing by the day. A recent development is that many young people are seeking asylum in the West.

While the situation is increasingly difficult, the church continues to spread the gospel of hope. Christians in Kosovo have just one important key in their hands: their own lives. Virtually all Evangelicals in Kosovo – who are almost all ex-Muslims – came to believe in Christ through an encounter with a Christian at some point in their lives.[10]

Fruitful Minority

The KPEC is especially active in the public sphere because of the formal freedom of religion and protection given by the law. In spite of setbacks and difficulties, the KPEC is serving God in the place where God has called

---

[10] See: F. Cakolli, ed., *The Hand of God: Faith Testimonies from the War in Kosova* (Prishtinë: Shtëpia Botuese Tenda, 2006).

it. It is a faithful church and perseveres in its ministry to God and the body of Christ in Kosovo. The KPEC sets an example of what it means to follow Christ and give public witness in times of subordination and social persecution.

In Western countries churches are usually free to serve God in the public sphere. They are free to establish (Christian) political parties. They can freely participate in debates in universities. They are allowed to publish in newspapers and journals. They can found Christian unions and large churches. We rejoice that Western churches can influence their societies. In turn, we ask them to empathise with the pain and distress that their brothers and sisters in other contexts experience, especially when they are excluded, discriminated or even persecuted.

Social persecution is a way of life for local Evangelical believers and churches in Kosovo. Yet many of them openly testify to their faith. Others are not (yet) ready for this step, but one thing is clear: God's work is ongoing in this small country, and the church is growing. Some will consider this growth to be slow, but the movement of this community, which has fellowship in the Crucified One, is of a continuous nature. While taking up their burdens and their cross they try to evangelize. Although they experience struggles and difficulties, they are a fruitful minority in the context of Islam.

For Further Reflection

Imagine that you are part of a church in a predominantly Islamic context. You face social persecution or, even worse, physical persecution. How do you think this would influence your church community and your personal faith? Think about positive and negative effects.

Quotation: 'I want to encourage the church of Kosovo never to forget what God has done for you, no matter what you go through. Think back and remember his faithfulness to you!'[11] This quote comes from a testimony of Artan, an ex-Muslim from Kosovo. What comes to your mind when you read this quote?

How do you read John 15:20 with the context of Kosovo in mind? "A servant is not greater than his master. If they persecuted me, they will persecute you also."

In general the churches in the West have to deal with shrinking churches and less involvement of their believers:

---

[11] F. Cakolli, *The Hand of God*, 18.

- If you are a Christian from the West: What can you and your church learn from the situation of Evangelical Christians in Kosovo in relation to the situation of churches in the West?
- If you are a Christian from another part of the world: What do you think that Western churches could learn from churches in the context of Islam?

Being a Christian with a Muslim Background

Some Notes Regarding Muslim Background Believers and the Dutch Churches

Herman Takken

This chapter addresses a very specific Christian community: that of believers with a Muslim background in the Netherlands. This group is a minority in their Muslim community, in the Christian church, and in society at large. They have needs, but they also have much to give to the church and to society.

Longing for Understanding

"I don't need a bag full of money, I don't need a pretentious sermon. I long for understanding, a hand on my shoulder, brotherly advice." This reaction of a Muslim background believer (MBB) characterises how these newcomers in faith, often with Oriental backgrounds, feel when they come to a Western country like the Netherlands. Meeting MBBs makes us, Dutch Christians, aware of our own culture in society and church. Is it strange that our brothers and sisters from the Middle East and North Africa feel alienated? Is it strange that they miss fellowship in an individualistic society and a church influenced by individualism? Many questions arise when we focus on MBBs and the Dutch churches. We can only touch on some of them here.

In dealing with MBBs and the Dutch churches we do not wish to focus exclusively on the MBB and his or her difficulties with the church. We also need to be aware of the problems that Dutch churches and Christians have with MBBs. In the same way, both "newcomers" and "established Christians" can testify that their encounters and their walk together are enriching. Before addressing that relation in more detail I will provide some general information on immigrants and refugees in the Netherlands.

Immigrants and Refugees in the Netherlands

Currently there are an estimated nine hundred thousand Muslims in the Netherlands, mainly from Turkey and Morocco. They came as guest workers some thirty to fifty years ago and in the course of time they brought their families to the Netherlands. More recently, many Muslim refugees from countries like Iran, Afghanistan, Somalia, Iraq and Syria (amongst them also some Christians) entered the country and obtained residency. Their cultural backgrounds and Islamic identity differs strongly from that of Turks and Moroccans. Quite often they have experienced exclusion, intolerance or even violence in name of Islam in their home countries. Inwardly, many among them have decided to leave Islam and search for a new religion to meet their religious needs. Dutch churches have welcomed many newcomers from Muslim backgrounds who left their countries in the Middle East, Asia or North Africa, and were baptized after some time.

It is of the greatest importance that these newcomers in Christian faith are discipled, so that they truly get to know the Lord Jesus and grow in faith, spiritually and practically. For many, the reason for becoming a Christian is the desire to leave Islam (push factor). The real reason for being a Christian should, however, be the attractiveness of Jesus as Lord and Saviour (pull factor). Jesus is the basis of faith and hence newcomers need to know him more and walk with him daily.

As for the migrants from Turkey and Morocco, most of them have found no reason to leave Islam. In fact, the Islamic identity of many among them was reinforced. Geopolitical developments involving Muslim countries and growing anti-Islamic sentiments have prompted them to take a clearer stand and articulate their Muslim faith. The number of MBBs from the Turkish and Moroccan communities in the Netherlands is, therefore, still very small. We estimate some hundreds.

Churches about MBBs

Churches that receive MBBs may become disappointed or even frustrated when MBBs do not respect appointments, fail to show gratitude or fail to acknowledge favours altogether, are too passive and rely heavily on others, expect support when again and again they have money problems, fall back into legalism or constant moral failure (with alcohol, in improper relationships etc.). These are not hypothetical cases, but real-life examples. When they, still Muslims, made contact with Christians and churches, the reason may have been to just profit from the relationship. If newcomers do not see the glory of Jesus Christ and the challenge in following him, the situation will become unbearable and lead to frustrations.

Fortunately there are many positive experiences too. A negative start and wrong motives may be overcome and lead to victory and growth in faith. Jesus' parable of the prodigal son shows a person who returned home with questionable motives. Eventually though, the relationship with his father was restored.

Many Dutch churches have been enriched by these brothers and sisters from culturally and religiously different backgrounds. Dutch Christians are impressed by the faith of their brothers and sisters, who sometimes have minimal knowledge of the Bible and the Christian faith, but a great faith in and dedication to their Lord and Saviour. They are like the Syro-Phoenician woman in Tyre to whom Jesus exclaims: "Woman, you have great faith."(Matt 15:28) Many of them are willing "to go the extra mile" and share what they have, in a way that makes Dutch Christians embarrassed.

MBBs and Churches

From the perspective of MBBs, the life of Dutch Christians is stiff and sober. "They rarely show any spontaneity. Everything is measured and calculated: time, money, meals. They are controlled more by their agendas rather than by their relationships. I always need to make an appointment early. Otherwise I create problems for my Dutch friends. They are so busy. Not many are willing to open their house, let alone to share their family life."

The MBB expects the new church to be a new family, in which there is understanding for his displacement and loneliness. He, an apostate, is rejected by and quite often expelled from his physical family. He longs for empathy and nearness from his new "brothers and sisters", a term he likes so much exactly because of these feelings. Will he travel his path of ups and downs, depression, feelings of shame and guilt, sometimes even satanic attack alone? Left to their own devices, many are unable to cope and will soon fall away from Christian faith.

Stages Leading up to Conversion

I am privileged to have three MBBs among my colleagues. One of them has written about the stages a MBB goes through before adopting the Christian faith. A Muslim who has contact with a Dutch Christian usually starts by defending Islam and trying to prove that Islam is the only true religion, arguing on the basis of facts and logic. In Islam, the way to please Allah is showing exemplary behaviour according to the model of the prophet Muhammad. When sharing his life with a Dutch Christian, a Muslim therefore often begins to question his own behaviour and starts thinking outside the box of traditional Islam. He comes up with questions about the Christian life and faith. What he hears and sees in the lives of Christian friends may impress him, but also shake his foundations. In this turbulent phase he may have conflicts with his Christian friends or avoid them altogether. Finally, a phase of searching and pondering sets in before the MBB comes to accept the Christian faith and enters a phase of spiritual growth.

Which Church Suits Best?

The nature of the phase after conversion depends on many factors. Two of these factors are the reaction of the old environment and the attitude of the new community. Many missionaries who work in Muslim communities have explored which church model is the most attractive and fitting for MBBs. The fact is that MBBs are welcomed and baptized in different denominations of the Dutch church. It is not so much the theology, structure or liturgy of a church which is decisive, but rather the warmth of hospitality and fellowship. Is there a person, or preferably a group of people, on whom MBBs can rely, not only on Sunday morning, but throughout the week? Are there brothers and sisters with sensitivity for the feelings of MBBs and the phases they go through? Are there spiritual fathers or mothers who help them to overcome hardship and depression, the results of being rejected by the old community? Is there anyone to disciple and shepherd them?

Irrespective of denomination, certain types of churches in the Netherlands are particularly hospitable to MBBs. This is especially true for some newly planted churches, such as the International Christian Fellowships. These communities pay specific attention to the cultural background and mother language of MBBs. They generally host more MBBs than traditional Dutch churches. Sadly, it appears to be hard for MBBs to sustain a long-term membership in traditional Dutch churches. After an enthusiastic start with high expectations of the new community, quite often they get disappointed. In such cases one could argue that perhaps their faith was in the flock of the Shepherd, rather than in the Good Shepherd himself. Nevertheless, churches that aspire to be permanent spiritual homes to MBBs need to involve them. Just like any active church member, MBBs as newcomers to churches need to be given tasks and be stimulated to bear responsibility and to take care of others. Above all, they need to grow in their faith in Jesus, not only on an emotional level, but also by serious Bible study and the discipline of daily quiet time.

A Reflection of the Universal Church

As we mentioned above, some newly planted churches with a culture open to MBBs' cultural patterns do better in this area. In various places in the Netherlands, mission workers have therefore started churches with such open, non-traditional cultures, separate from the established, traditional Dutch churches. However, separate churches with a specific culture and a specific language may be not the best long-term solution to MBBs. What about their children who grow up in a Western country? Won't they prefer to be part of a more mainstream Dutch church community? And more importantly, is receiving converts into existing churches not a reflection of the biblical vision of the universal church, described in the heavenly vision in the Book of Revelation, which includes all tribes and nations? Therefore, it would be better to integrate this wave of new believers into existing churches. This requires a willingness on the part of the churches in the Netherlands and in other Western countries to make changes and create a church with greater diversity.[12] Are these established churches prepared to make such changes?

We can also imagine a combination of the two solutions: a middle ground where MBBs and established churches encounter each other, while maintaining a safe place to withdraw. One could think of joint Sunday morning services, followed by fellowship groups with Christians from similar backgrounds. In this way biblical unity across borders can be experienced, yet people can also enjoy fellowship with their own traditions, culture and language. The culture-specific times of fellowship may include a meal, Bible study, praying and singing in one's own language.

Those Who Have Crossed Over

We use the term MBB for lack of a better one. This term is used worldwide to denote a Christian with a Muslim background. But MBB is a rather clinical abbreviation, which MBBs themselves do not like. In the Arabic world they speak amongst themselves of 'aberin, pilgrims, literally "those who have crossed" a border or barrier and gone from Islam into

---

12   E.M. Hicham, MBB from North Africa and writer of several books e.g. *Your Questions Answered: A Reply to Muslim Friends*. See http://www.word-of-hope.net.

the light of Christ. This term fits their situation and has a deep meaning because of the biblical connotation. Abram was called a Hebrew (Gen 14:13), as were Joseph (Gen 39:14 and 41:12) and the people of Israel (Exod 1:15-16). Although the origin of the word is not fully certain, we can speak of *'aberin* as "strangers and pilgrims on the earth". The expression comes from the Book of Hebrews. The writer says of Abraham: "By faith he made his home in the promised land like a stranger in a foreign country; he lived in tents . . . For he was looking forward to the city with foundations, whose architect and builder is God' (Heb 11:9-10). This chapter is encouraging and appealing to our *'aberin* brothers and sisters, who also "passed the Red Sea by faith" (Heb 11:29) and are in comparable situations.

Sword and Shield

The Armenian Evangelical Churches in the Middle East

Wilbert van Saane

This chapter highlights the role of the Armenian Evangelical Churches in the Middle East. It sketches the history of Armenian Christianity and its interaction with predominantly Muslim nations. It focuses on the continuing witness and service of the Armenian Evangelicals, who form a small minority within the Armenian communities in the Middle East.

The First Christian Nation

According to tradition, the apostles Thaddaeus and Bartholomew brought the good news of Jesus Christ to Armenia. A few centuries later, Armenia was the first nation to accept Christianity as a state religion. We know from Eusebius and other ancient sources that by the mid-third century there were churches across different parts of Armenia. The missionary work of Gregory the Illuminator and a miraculous healing eventually led to the conversion of King Trdat III, most probably in the year 301. The king's conversion was a turning point for the whole nation. Upon royal decree, all of Armenia adopted Christianity. Christianity has been an inalienable part of the Armenian national identity ever since, especially as embodied by the Armenian Apostolic Church.

Armenians under the Sword

Since the seventh century, the Armenian Church had to define itself vis-à-vis Islam. In 641, Arab troops captured the capital of the nation, killed the head of the Armenian Church and slayed around twelve thousand Armenians. It was the first of many conquests of Armenia by Muslim powers. After the Caliphate, the Seljuk Turks, the Ottomans and the Safavid Persians fought over parts of Armenia, until finally in the nineteenth century Western Armenia – today's Eastern Anatolia – fell under the Ottoman Empire while Eastern Armenia was in Russian hands.

The weakening Ottoman Empire looked for a scapegoat and found it in the Armenians. An estimated one-and-a-half million Armenians perished in the massacres, deportations and resulting famines. The survivors of the Armenian genocide went into exile to parts of the Middle East, Eastern Armenia or the Western world. In the years after the genocide, the Armenian diaspora grew significantly.

Paradoxically, instead of destroying it, the genocide only strengthened the Armenian resolve and identity. Post-genocide Armenians were determined to preserve their faith and culture in the midst of overwhelmingly Muslim societies. It is primarily in the great urban centres of the Near East – such as Tehran, Isfahan, Baghdad, Aleppo, Beirut, Istanbul, Jerusalem, Cairo and Alexandria – that the diaspora Armenians continued to be a fruitful Christian presence.

The Early History of Armenian Protestantism

The Armenian Evangelical churches have their roots in the first half of the nineteenth century. In Constantinople, a spiritual renewal started *within* the Apostolic Church. A group of lay people and clergy devoted themselves to prayer and Bible reading, hoping to renew the Church. At around the same time, Western Bible Societies made efforts to provide new Bible translations and Western Protestant missionaries came to preach the gospel in the Near East.

The missionaries found natural allies in the revivalist Armenians. The growth of the number of "Evangelicals" alarmed the leaders of the Apostolic Church. Years of fierce conflict followed and eventually the revivalist group was forced out of the Apostolic Church and began the Armenian Evangelical Church (1846).

Protestantism proved an innovative and emancipatory force among Ottoman Armenians, especially in the field of education. Many were attracted to the new denomination. By the beginning of the twentieth century, it was a community of around sixty thousand people, spread over 137 congregations concentrated mostly in Western Armenia. In the first half century of their existence, the Armenian Evangelicals established a network of around four hundred schools that served Armenians from all denominations. The transformative impact of these schools, where the Bible was at the centre, can hardly be overstated.

The Ottoman authorities acknowledged Armenian Protestants as a separate denomination, or *millet*. This means that they were allowed to build their own churches, schools and other institutions. The government also gave them jurisdiction in matters of family law. The glorious decades of growth of Armenian Evangelicalism ended in the genocide, which was survived by only fifteen out of the sixty thousand Protestants in the Ottoman Empire. After the fall of the Ottoman Empire, the millet system was continued in different forms throughout the Near East, securing a certain degree of freedom for Christian minorities, including Armenian Evangelicals.

The Post-Genocide Armenian Diaspora

To the Armenian diaspora in the Middle East, the twentieth century was a story of gradual emancipation and, later, of fast decline. Out of the horrors of the genocide, the impoverished surviving Armenians silently rebuilt a modest and respectable middle class life. As newcomers in their host communities, many chose "free" occupations; they became craftsmen and traders, or went into agriculture and the food business.

Through their reliability, modesty and hard work, the Armenian diaspora communities steadily gained the respect of their host communities. The Armenians, for their part, generally felt welcomed in Syria, Jordan, Lebanon, Egypt, Iran and Iraq. An attitude of appreciation towards these nations that took them in prevailed. Gradually, they began to contribute to the modernization of their nations, particularly during the decades following World War II. At the time most Near Eastern countries were under modernizing and secularist, albeit sometimes despotic, governments. This gave Armenians the chance to establish schools, medical facilities and cultural institutions.

Since the 1970s, the Armenian presence in the Middle East rapidly diminished. The factors for that vary from country to country. The violence of the Lebanese Civil War (1975-1991) prompted many Lebanese to leave, but the Armenian community lost relatively more than any other community: some scholars estimate that it dwindled from two hundred thousand before the war to one hundred thousand after the war. Today that number is probably somewhat higher due to the influx of Syrian Armenians.

The Iranian Revolution (1979) led to a complete transformation of the country and a radically different position for the Christians. During the war with Iraq, many Armenians served in the Iranian army and gave their life for their country. After that, however, the number of Armenians continued to decline due to emigration. It is difficult to find reliable estimates of the number of Armenians in Iran; perhaps they number around one hundred-fifty thousand.

In Iraq and Syria, Armenians enjoyed a reasonably peaceful and prosperous existence, until the American invasion of Iraq (2003) and the changes in the wake of the Arab Spring. The violence in these countries has decimated their Armenian communities. It is estimated that in Aleppo, which before the war had the largest concentration of Syrian Armenians (around sixty thousand), only seven-and-a-half thousand Armenians remain. In all of Syria there are perhaps twenty-five thousand Armenians left, only a quarter of the pre-war number of one hundred thousand. The current Armenian population of Iraq is no larger than ten thousand and possibly much smaller than that.

Compared to the surrounding nations, the Armenian communities of Jordan (around three thousand) and Egypt (around six thousand) did not experience as much political upheaval, but they too declined due to emigration.

Armenian Evangelical Witness and Service Today

In all these countries, a small group of Armenian Evangelicals have remained. In what ways do they witness to their faith today? And in what ways are they committed to service in the footsteps of Jesus Christ? In what ways are they a fruitful minority in the Middle East?

On the individual level, many Armenian Evangelicals witness to their faith on a daily basis. Although in some areas Armenians have formed ghettos, in most towns and cities they live in mixed Christian-Muslim neighbourhoods. And although Armenian culture may be described as quite introverted, good neighbourly relations are of the highest value. The diaspora Armenian community knows better than anyone else that one's life may depend on a good neighbour. Friendships and cooperation with Muslims are therefore encouraged among Armenian Evangelicals.

Neighbourliness is of equal importance to the Armenian Evangelical Churches. The relations between the Armenian Evangelical Churches and the Armenian Catholic and Apostolic Churches is much improved since the excommunication of the first Protestants in the nineteenth century. Armenian Evangelicals were pioneers in ecumenism in the Middle East. Today the different Armenian denominations maintain close ties and cooperate in various ways. They all participate in the Middle East Council of Churches. The current wave of violence in Syria and Iraq has brought them even closer together. They realize they cannot afford to be divided in the face of the threats to their future in the region.

Armenian Evangelical Churches also do what they can to promote cordial relations with Islamic leaders and communities. At the local level, they look for practical cooperation, especially in threatened and deprived parts of Syria, where water, food supplies, medical care and other basic necessities are shared. At the level of national churches, Armenian Evangelicals engage in dialogue with Islamic leaders and scholars. Wherever the Armenians still have representatives in local or national politics, they contribute to initiatives that promote stability and peaceful coexistence.

Historically, Armenian Evangelicals have been pioneers in education and today they still uphold that tradition. In Syria and Lebanon the Armenian Evangelical Churches still run a dozen or so primary and secondary schools. In the other Middle Eastern countries, this has become impossible for a variety of reasons. The burden of the educational institutions falls on the shoulders of a handful of qualified and highly committed Armenian Evangelicals. In Beirut, Haigazian University is an institution for higher learning with a distinctly Protestant and Armenian character. Unlike the Evangelical primary and secondary schools, which are exclusively Armenian, Haigazian University has a mixed student body and also employs Muslims. It is a place where peaceful coexistence between the religions is practised, while at the same time the Christian message is communicated with respect to the other faith traditions. Apart from providing quality training in different majors, Haigazian is an important centre for the academic study of the Armenian diaspora. With several other denominations, the Armenian Evangelical Churches also maintain the Near East School of Theology, where pastors and church leaders receive their training.

Finally, the Armenian Evangelical Churches of the Middle East also engage in social and medical work. The Social Action Committee oversees a number of ministries in Syria and Lebanon, among which are relief work, social work, retirement homes, care for mentally disabled people, and a dental and basic health care clinic in Aleppo. In partnership with the Apostolic Church, the Evangelicals operate the CAHL home for the elderly and the Azounieh Sanatorium, which specialized in the treatment of tuberculosis. Although these services are primarily directed towards Armenians, they also benefit others.

The Shield of the Armenian Language and Culture

The Armenian identity, culture and language have often functioned as a shield. Armenians are not Arabs, nor are they Persians. Very few Arabs and very few Iranians speak the Armenian language. This has made the Armenians a very distinct group, with an exceptional position in the Middle East. Because they are so different, they do not constitute a threat to the status quo. For that reason, governments have often given them considerable freedom, or even enlisted their support. The notable exception was of course the crumbling Ottoman Empire in the late nineteenth and early twentieth century. Even in post-revolution Iran, the Armenian churches have generally been allowed to practise their faith, as long as they refrained from religious involvement with Persian speakers.

This shield has given the Armenian minorities across the Middle East considerable freedom to manoeuvre. It has enabled them to preserve their faith – embedded in their national identity. It has given them the opportunity to faithfully work and witness as Christians.

A shield is for defence and securing continuity. Perhaps an overly defensive attitude has been the weakness of Armenian communities in the Middle East, including the Armenian Evangelical Churches. Many have withdrawn into their national identity, their language, and their culture – making the bridge between non-Armenians and Armenians and between non-Christians and Christians nearly impassable. With the history of violence against Armenians in mind, however, this shielding mechanism is understandable.

Today the existence of the Armenian community in the Middle East, including the Evangelicals among them, is threatened by the sword of war yet again. This is a sad fact and may at times lead us to question the divine wisdom behind the events we are witnessing. It is vital that Christians all over the world show solidarity with the Armenians in their current predicament, as well as with other religious minorities in the Middle East. The history of Armenians in the Islamic world should, however, also give us hope: it teaches us that where a faithful Christian presence is forcibly ended in one place, by God's grace it re-emerges and bears fruit in another place. It reminds us that God "is a shield for all who take refuge in him" (Ps 18:30 NRSV).

Conclusion

Wilbert van Saane

This concluding chapter will highlight some points that the different chapters have in common. First, the common challenges that are raised by the different authors will be described. Second, the ways to overcome those challenges that were proposed in the different chapters will be revisited. Third, this chapter also brings together the biblical and theological inspiration for Christian minorities that the authors have offered. Finally, at the end of this chapter, a subject will be raised that has not featured prominently in any of the chapters: the role of Muslim communities in supporting and cooperating with Christian minorities. So, looking back on the contributions of a dozen or so authors, what can be said about the fruitfulness of minority communities in predominantly Islamic contexts?

The Challenges

Christian minorities in Islamic societies face manifold challenges. If there is one thing this book makes clear, it is this point. The challenges present themselves on several levels. Some of the most formidable trials of Christian minorities are in fact caused by the governments of the countries they live in. In areas such as Central Asia, the Balkans and North Africa registration of churches has been problematic to say the least. As various authors have demonstrated, registration of a religious community means much more than just having the name of your church in the books and enjoying an official status. It makes it possible for Christian churches to purchase properties, provide their members with cemeteries and Christian burial rites, perform weddings and the like. Registration also gives Christians a ground of appeal in case their freedom of religion is violated. The stories of the Evangelical churches in Albania and Algeria, which both achieved a degree of official state recognition, are encouraging examples for churches that still seek to be acknowledged.

The presumed "foreignness" of Christianity often proves an obstacle on the path to official recognition. It is therefore important that Christians across the Muslim world familiarize themselves with the long history of the church in their region – Christian presence often predates Muslim presence – and communicate this history in a positive way to show that Christianity belongs to their countries as much as Islam does. This may help Christians who are culturally overwhelmed and find it hard to maintain their identity as Christians in a predominantly Islamic society.

Another challenge for Christian minorities is to gain the trust of Muslim spiritual leaders. A dismissive or outright hostile attitude on the part of some Muslim clergy has harmed Christian minorities across the world. Examples of this have been described in the chapters about Central Asia and Albania, where individual Muslim leaders posed a threat to churches and individual Christians. In places where Christians have been able to build relationships of trust with Muslim leaders, they have often been protected and given freedom to worship. The story of the interreligious firefighting at the church in Egypt illustrates this point well.

Evangelical Christians often encounter hostility from Muslim leaders and communities because they evangelize. It is part and parcel of the Evangelical faith to communicate the gospel as the message of salvation for everybody. For Evangelicals this is a matter of love and concern for one's neighbour. However, Muslims often fail to see this and perceive evangelism as a deceptive and ill-intentioned way of undermining the Muslim community, the *umma*. When individual Muslims are on the verge of conversion, their fellow-Muslims are likely to interpret this as a defeat and threat to their community. This explains hostile reactions to Evangelical churches across the Muslim world. Evangelizing Christians need to be transparent about their motives and sincere in their methods of evangelism to overcome the distrust. Any form of coercion or manipulation in evangelism must be avoided, not only because it understandably offends Muslims, but also because it betrays the very message Christians are preaching.

In addition to their concern for the integrity of the *umma*, many Muslims view conversion out of Islam as apostasy, a sin which may lead to punishment. This was the reason why Saudi Arabia did not sign the Universal Declaration of Human Rights, which included the freedom to change one's religion – a proposal of the Lebanese scholar Charles Malik.

Because conversion is tantamount to apostasy it is no wonder that many Muslim families struggle so much when one of their own leaves what is in their eyes the plain truth for a corrupted and morally inferior religion. In interfaith dialogue these sensitive issues can be explored and Christians and Muslims can come to a deeper understanding of the pain and the joy involved in conversion. In such dialogues Christians will insist that Islam too must grant the freedom to change one's faith.

Finally, an increasing problem of Christian minorities is violence and terror inflicted on them by Islamist groups like ISIS, al-Nusra and al-Qaeda. The rise of such groups has causes that are political rather than religious and are only marginally related to Christianity, but nonetheless they tend to scapegoat religious minorities and do not hesitate to torture, abuse and kill people whose beliefs differ from theirs. In their eyes, Christians are infidels and representatives of Western power. As a result, churches have become the targets of bombings, Christian communities have been displaced, groups of Christians have been held hostage, Christian women have been used as sex slaves and Christian clergy have been killed. This has not only happened in Iraq and Syria, but in other countries as well. It is only a very small group of Muslims that engages in such terrorist activities and the vast majority of Muslims insists that their behaviour is not in accordance with Islam, but in recent years these few have done severe harm to the religious minorities living in Muslim lands. Central governments have struggled to protect their citizens from such violence.

Ways to Be a Fruitful Minority

All the authors of this book agree that Christian minorities should engage with their societies as much as they can and not withdraw. They agree that Christians should not have an attitude of quiet resignation and passively accept their fate, come what may. They also believe that Christians should not fall into the trap of rejecting and fighting off anything that happens in their societies. To borrow a metaphor from the Lebanese scholar Martin Accad, Christians should be neither like chameleons nor like hedgehogs. In case of danger the chameleon changes colour and becomes almost invisible, whereas the hedgehog rolls into a tight ball and makes its spines point outwards. It is not in assimilation nor in withdrawal, but in the engagement with their societies that Christian minorities become fruitful minorities, the writers of the different chapters argue.

A fruitful engagement with any society begins with an understanding of the way that society thinks and functions. For Christians in predominantly Muslim countries this means they have to acquaint themselves not only with the constitution and "secular" legislation of their country, but also with Islamic jurisprudence. Both systems of law have implications for their status and freedom as a minority. It is also helpful to analyse society on a deeper level, as Petrus Sugito does in his chapter, pointing out that the majority may also suffer from a minority complex or be moved by fear and painful memories; and as Najla Kassab does, demonstrating that the prevailing understanding of power in Islamic societies is different from Jesus' understanding of power.

In order to yield spiritual fruit Christians need to stay rooted in their faith and continue to give witness of that faith. This is an insight that recurs in all the chapters of this book. A living faith is a faith that expresses itself in words and in acts. It cannot remain silent or unnoticed, not even in prison, when kidnapped or under threat. Many chapters also emphasize that witness is given in full respect of other religions and convictions, especially Islam. As they witness, Christians do not seek to alienate or offend others. As a recent document jointly issued by the World Evangelical Alliance, the World Council of Churches and the Pontifical Council for Interreligious Dialogue has it: "For Christians it is a joy and a privilege to give an accounting for the hope that is within them and to do so with gentleness and respect." (*Christian Witness in a Multi-Religious World: Recommendations for Conduct*)

A fruitful Christian community is not only a community that reaches out in witness, but also a community that is pastoral, hospitable and willing to receive. The doors of the churches should be open to all and the community should be willing to accommodate guests, seekers, people who are abandoned and people who inquire and decide to stay indeterminately. Several chapters underline the importance of this and point out that extending hospitality means taking risks and requires self-denial, even in a country like the Netherlands, as Herman Takken demonstrates in his chapter.

Service to society, diaconal care and relief work are also ways in which Christian minorities bear fruit. In times of war and crisis, a readiness and swiftness to serve is of particular importance. In the Egyptian revolution the churches cared for the injured. In the Syrian crisis the churches are offering relief and education to those who are deprived of it. In Indonesia a refugee community was able to turn its fate and became a giving community. And of course there are numerous other examples that could be mentioned. In its service, Christian communities need to be aware of the needs of their societies and creatively try to meet those needs. If they do, as Najla Kassab argues, Christian minorities can be change-makers and bridge-builders in their societies.

Some authors recommend that Christian minorities should become more engaged in the politics of their countries. In many countries in the Muslim world, Christians do not have that freedom. Where that freedom exist, these authors state, Christians should not withdraw in a cocoon, but should use the opportunities to be active members of political parties, to lobby, to help govern and by their exposure to demonstrate the pluralism of society. By their courageous political involvement the churches in Albania, Kosovo, Algeria and Egypt have booked some progress in recent years. As other authors remind us, however, Christian communities are still on the side lines of politics in many other countries. Other authors offer a reminder that siding with a political party may be dangerous, and may also obscure the belief that God's kingdom is not found in a certain political stance, but is in fact above all.

Biblical and Theological Resources for Fruitful Minorities

As they strive to be fruitful in their respective societies, Christian communities in Muslim contexts can draw courage and inspiration from the Bible and from Christian theology. The authors of the first four chapters lead the reader through a treasure of biblical and theological resources that speak to minority communities. What these chapters also do is redefine the concept of minority as something positive. Paradoxically, as minorities Christian communities are able to impact society in a more powerful way, because in the weakness and vulnerability of his followers the power of Christ is revealed.

Atef Gendy, Najla Kassab, Bernhard Reitsma and Petrus Sugito all stress the path of vulnerability that Jesus walked and that Christian communities are called to walk after him. For Jesus, this path led to the cross, where he emptied himself for others. For Christians, this path may lead to suffering as well, but it may also help them to discover their calling in the societies that they are part of. As Kassab writes: "A minority group that accepts its minority status is automatically triggered to serve others outside its borders."

It is not only the cross that inspires and moves Christians who live as minorities in predominantly Muslim societies. It is also the resurrection life which manifests itself in their communities and makes them eschatological communities and communities of hope. In the face of current suffering, Christians can still have hope and, as Gendy writes, "actively participate in transforming the current frustrating hopeless situation into a hopeful one".

The authors of this book also agree that the minority status of Christians in Islamic countries helps them become creative communities. Christian minorities can, as Kassab writes, serve as laboratories. As small minorities they are mobile and pliable. They are more like a small aircraft than like a large Jumbo Jet. The changes they propose and pioneer may not have an immediate impact on society at large, but they are significant and may eventually result in a renewal of considerable segments of society. They are stars amidst the darkness, the light of the world, the salt of the earth.

International Partnerships

Most Christian communities in Islamic countries have connections with Christians in other parts of the world. They are part of informal transnational networks and formal fellowships and councils of churches. To many, being part of such networks is a source of encouragement and support. In hard times it helps them to know that there are others who pray for them and who are willing to support them. These networks are also communities of learning, in which the experience of a church in one place can help a church in another place.

International partnerships have their limits. For instance, in spite of all the advocacy and lobbying efforts the World Council of Churches and the World Evangelical Alliance have not been able to turn the tide for the now decimated churches in Iraq and Syria. Also, in totalitarian countries that strictly censor and monitor their communication networks Christians have been not been able to communicate freely with their partners in other countries.

Still, the value of such partnerships is inestimable. They give expression to the unity of the church worldwide. They provide Christian minorities with a "home" when their home countries are hostile to them. They are "places" where the stories of struggling brothers and sisters are heard and where pastoral care is provided. If possible, representatives of international church networks and councils can visit Christian minorities and encourage them. They can appeal to international authorities when they hear that their member churches suffer injustice. They can put outside pressure on governments to grant minority communities freedom of religion. The example given in this book is the involvement of the World Evangelical Alliance in the registration of the Evangelical Church of Albania.

Muslim Majorities and Fruitful Christian Minorities

Throughout the centuries, Christians have been fruitful minorities in Muslim majority contexts. Examples that are often highlighted are the Assyrian Christian scholars at the Abbasid court of Baghdad and the Armenians who continued their high-standing culture within the Ottoman Empire. Muslim rulers and societies have often gratefully received the gifts offered by the Christian minorities living among them. Today, Christian minorities in Islamic societies long for freedom and peace so that they can be fruitful and contribute to the economies, the political life, and the cultures of these societies. Many Muslims also long for peaceful coexistence between Muslims and Christians and realize that the disappearance of Christian minorities from their societies would mean a loss.

Predominantly Muslim nations continuously face the question how to balance sharia law with secular systems of government, be it democracy, monarchy, totalitarianism or other forms of administration. For the nations that are emerging from the dust of the revolutions and wars in the Middle East this question is particularly pertinent. At this point in time it is clear that both the "old" countries and the newly emerging countries will have a government that is less secular in nature than their predecessors. Until recently only few countries claimed to have an Islamic constitution: Afghanistan, Saudi Arabia, Iran and three or four others. The Islamic State has joined this select group and more states may follow. They will rely more on their Islamic sources for their governing and legislative structures. This means they will probably review the position of religious minorities more in light of Islamic law than in light of the principles of a multicultural secular state. In some cases, this might mean a return to the principles of the dhimma, as we are seeing in the Islamic State in Iraq and Syria. Christian minorities will find it difficult to remain loyal to countries that will treat them as dhimmis and will migrate away from these areas if they have the chance. Over the past years this has happened in Iraq and Syria, where the Christian presence has been weakened significantly.

Fortunately for Christians and other religious minorities, there are many Muslim scholars who do not believe the dhimma should be reinforced today. They believe it is a system that was appropriate in the time of the Prophet, but not today. They propose other relations between the Muslim majority and the non-Muslim minorities which feature the concept of citizenship and seek to harmonize human rights with Islamic laws.

The violence of terrorist groups in their countries and the resulting disappearance of religious minorities is a source of concern for many Muslims today. In January 2016 a group of over two hundred-fifty scholars met in the Moroccan city of Marrakech on the occasion of the fourteen hundredth anniversary of the Medina Charter, the treaty in which the Prophet Muhammad arranged the position of religious minorities when Islam became the official religion of his new state. These leaders from across the Muslim world showed their deep concern about the widespread violence in their countries. Significantly, they declared that in their view the Medina Charter is in harmony with the Universal Declaration of Human Rights. They affirmed the need for interreligious cooperation to counter the threats that face humanity today and the need for full protection of the rights and liberties of all religious groups. They called Muslim scholars around the world to develop jurisprudence around the idea of inclusive citizenship and revisions of educational curricula that promote aggression and violence. They also advocated "a broad movement for the just treatment of minorities in Muslim countries" and pointed out that all religions, sects and denominations should strive to respect what others hold sacred and to end hateful language. They ended their statement by affirming that "it is unconscionable to employ religion for the purpose of aggressing upon the rights of religious minorities in Muslim countries".

There is much that Muslim communities can do to ensure that religious minorities remain part of their societies. In the same way, there is much that Christian communities can do to help Muslim minorities thrive outside the Muslim world. Such mutual assistance and protection does not mean that either Christians or Muslims have to compromise their faith, nor does it mean that mutual witness is no longer possible. On the contrary, if Christians and Muslims are transparent to each other and work for each other's wellbeing, they will be much more likely to discover each other's deepest convictions and sources of inspiration.

Faith and Hope

As they wait and pray for Muslim societies to become more tolerant and hospitable to minorities, Christians must faithfully continue to live their lives of discipleship. The first edition of Kenneth Cragg's book *The Call of the Minaret* (1956) ended with a chapter entitled "The Call to Patience". In later editions Cragg chose to give his chapter the title "The Call to Faith and Hope". On that note I would also like to end this chapter. Farmers need to wait patiently for the fruit of their efforts, but above all they need to be faithful and diligent in tending their crops, filled with hope that they will produce an abundant harvest in due season. The Christian life is like that, as the New Testament suggests in different places. The patience of Christians living in Islamic countries is at times severely tested by suffering and by the delay of the harvest. Many Christians have become discouraged and have chosen to move away from their homelands to the formerly Christian world to build new, and in their eyes more fruitful, lives for themselves. Many others have chosen to stay in Muslim lands, trusting that they may bear some fruit there. As the authors of this book have shown, some of this fruit is already being harvested and there is good reason to hope for a much greater harvest.